An Immigrant Church No Longer:

Reshaping Youth Ministry for Coptic Churches in North America

An Immigrant Church No Longer:

Reshaping Youth Ministry for Coptic Churches in North America

Shereen Marcus, J.D., M.A.

AGORA
UNIVERSITY
PRESS
EST. 2012

An Immigrant Church No Longer: Reshaping Youth Ministry for Coptic Churches in North America

Copyright © 2020 by Agora University Press

All rights reserved. Printed in the United States of America. No part of this book may be used or reproduced in any manner whatsoever without written permission except in the case of brief quotations embodied in critical articles or reviews.

For information contact: aupress@agora.edu
Agora University Press: https://press.agora.edu

ISBN: 978-1-950831-23-4

HIS HOLINESS POPE TAWADROS II
118th Pope and Patriarch of the great city of Alexandria and the See of St. Mark

HIS HOLINESS PATRIARCH IGNATIUS APHREM II
Patriarch of Antioch and All the East

PRINTED IN THE UNITED STATES OF AMERICA

"Assuredly, I say to you, unless you are converted and become as little children, you will by no means enter the Kingdom of Heaven."

Matthew 18:3

I dedicate this book to Christ and His words to us all to be converted and become as little children; to my husband who is my rock and supporter; my children who show me Christ everyday with their unconditional love; and to all the youth I serve because they teach me more than I can ever hope to teach them.

Acknowledgments

I am grateful to all the clergy and professors who devoted their time and efforts in instructing me at the Antiochian House of Studies. I am thankful for their guidance, constructive feedback, and support throughout the course of my studies and research for this book. In particular, I want to thank Very Rev. Dr. Joseph Purpura for his time spent sharing his lifelong experience in youth ministry, providing numerous resources, and giving me invaluable guidance on my material along the way. I also would like to thank H.G. Bishop Youssef, Fr. Anthony Messeh, and Fr. Daniel Hanna, for giving me their time to interview them about their youth ministry efforts and thoughts as they pertain to the Coptic Churches in North America.

Table of Contents

Introduction..8

Coptic Youth Ministry in North America Today..12

Sunday School Curriculum...................................25

Proposed Framework for Youth Ministry:

Koulomizin's Five Prongs....................................34

Conclusion..98

Appendices...102

Bibliography...141

About the Author...148

Introduction

The Coptic Orthodox immigration to North America was a relatively recent event, starting in Toronto (1964), Los Angeles (1969), and Jersey City (1970), and picking up momentum thereafter in the 1970s.[1] As such, the landscape within the North American Coptic Orthodox churches is unique and challenging, especially concerning the youth. As the Church developed, there emerged a mix of Egyptian-born and American-born congregants across all age brackets and within individual families. As the

---

[1] Fr. Michael Sorial, *Incarnational Exodus* (Saint Cyril of Alexandria Society Press, 2014), 2; Bishop Youssef, *Adapting to A New Place Called Home* (Texas: St. Mary & St. Moses Abbey Press, 2016).

Church progressed even further, the mix now includes non-Egyptian converts. There are invariably unique strengths and unique challenges that come with such a diverse mix. Many immigrants, for example, cling to their faith and church, wanting familiarity as they maneuver a new culture. With regard to youth ministry, the mix also causes clashes and barriers between the American-born youth and their immigrant parents with no real blueprint on how to bridge the gap. The response from the Coptic Church with respect to the youth has largely been focused on the traditional Sunday school programs, which is a great first step, but an incomplete view of youth ministry. Youth ministry in North America should be directed to helping young minds form their own personal faith in God and identity in the Body of Christ and maneuver through the moral and ethical issues they face in adolescences. Forming a partnership with parents, youth ministry should be the place where youth find solid foundation and support as they attempt to find their faith in an American secular world. An ancient faith was brought to an unfamiliar, modern world. Christ, however, is timeless and therefore relevant to all generations, to all cultures, to all families. This book explores the youth ministry development in the Coptic Orthodox churches in North America and what are proposed next steps to further reach the needs of the young Coptic Orthodox Christians in North America. In particular, there are two main problems with the current youth ministry structure in the Coptic Orthodox churches in North America: (1) Framework: there is no consistent framework to assist individual parishes develop a well-rounded youth ministry effort in their church; and (2) Curriculum: there is no uniform source to pull resources and/or curriculum materials from that is both theologically sound and age appropriate for the youth in North America.[2]

---

[2] Fr. Anthony Messeh, interview by author, Arlington, VA, June 14, 2018 (indicating there are some limited resources

The mission of any youth ministry should be to help facilitate individual faith in a young mind so that as they mature, their Christian faith is personalized, chosen, and an integral part of their lives. Fulfilling that mission in an immigrant church context requires some deliberate refocusing of the Coptic youth ministry format to fit the American-born youth. Rather than cater to the ethnic traditions that some cling to and take comfort in, the Coptic Orthodox parishes in North America, especially in the context of youth ministry, should focus on a "Christocentric cultural model" focusing on bringing the Christian life and the Christian message in a North American cultural context that today's Orthodox youth can find applicable and uplifting.[3]

---

available if you look for them, but no set guidelines with regard to Youth Ministry); Bishop Youssef, interview by author, Orlando, FL, June 2, 2018 (indicating every parish/diocese are largely able to create whatever curriculum they want); Fr. Daniel Hanna, interview by author, Warren, NJ, September 18, 2018.

[3] Sorial, *Incarnational Exodus*, 12-13 (discussing the importance of Christocentric culture versus "selfishly enjoying ...ethnic traditions...which America does not

Coptic Youth Ministry in North America Today

Youth ministry in Egypt versus in North American Coptic parishes looks very different.[4] In Egypt, Sunday school and youth ministry do not exist the same way they do in North America. Rather, Church is open seven days a week and specifically caters to the Christian community in a Muslim-dominated country.[5] Churches, outside of liturgical services,

---

understand." The author deems this Christocentric culture model imperative to the survival of the Orthodox Church in North America).

[4] Nader Tadros and Amy Ekdawi, interview by author, Fairfax, VA, March 22, 2018 (addressing their experience leading youth groups in Egypt under Bishop Moussa in the 1970s and 1980s).

[5] Youssef, *Adapting to A New Place Called Home*, 8 (talking about the fact that Christians in Egypt have always been the minority and never did rule their own country); *see also* Tadros and Ekdawi, interview.

operate as Country Club, Sports Club, Fellowship Club, and Spiritual Club all rolled into one.[6] Indeed, the early Church model included gatherings for both worship and fellowship.[7]

In North America, the first Coptic churches in the late 1960s and early 1970s clustered in cities in California and New Jersey by largely immigrants with professional degrees looking to escape the Muslim-dominated politics of Egypt and find a better life for their children.[8] Youth ministry in these first churches consisted solely of a traditional "Sunday school program" initially designed by an archdeacon, St. Habib

---

[6] Mai Shams El-Din, "Copts and Egypt's National Game: We'll Call You Back Later," *Navigate* (July 20, 2017), https://www.madamasr.com/en/2017/07/20/feature/society/copts-and-egypts-national-game-well-call-you-back-later/ (accessed December 11, 2017) (discussing how the Coptic Churches in Egypt had to develop sports clubs because must community clubs do not allow Christians to participate).

[7] See Acts 2:44 (NKJV) ("And all that believed were together, and had all things in common.").

[8] Youssef, *Adapting to A New Place Called Home*, 10-12.

Guirguis (canonized as a saint in June 2013).[9] There was no proactive plan at this point for youth ministry, just a designed Sunday school program by an archdeacon to meet the needs of the small community. Currently, the Coptic Church has a "Youth Bishophric" led by the Bishop of Youth, Bishop Moussa, with a vision of youth ministry for the Coptic Orthodox parishes. Specifically, his vision is to encourage individual parishes to mentor and disciple the youth with the foresight that these are the current and future leaders of the Church.[10] The youth were also a big concern for the Coptic Pope, His Holiness Pope Shenouda III. He would give general direction to the clergy to not forget the youth saying, "A church without youth, is a church without a future."[11] He also played a role in the creation of the summer competition program known as

---

[9] Ibid., 13-14; *see also* Bishop Suriel, *Habib Girgis: Coptic Educator and a Light in the Darkness* (New York: St. Vladimir's Seminary Press, 2017), Ch. 3.
[10] Youth Bishopric, "Mission Statement," http://youthbishopric.com/ (accessed August 14, 2018).
[11] Messeh, interview.

"Mahragan Al Keraza."[12] Bishop Moussa's work is largely concentrated in Egypt because that is where the Coptic population is largely concentrated.[13] While he is known in North America, has presented in conferences in North America, and has had books translated into English, the North American Coptic Orthodox parishes have a lot of independence to develop their own youth ministry vision.[14] As explained in an interview with Bishop Youssef, however, this is not the ideal as each diocese or congregation will have fragmented visions.[15] Rather, it would be a good long-term goal to have an Archdiocese

---

[12] Coptic Orthodox Diocese of Los Angeles, Southern California, and Hawaii, "About Us / Mahragan Al Keraza." http://www.ysc-keraza.org/about-us/mahragan-al-keraza/ (accessed Sept. 10, 2018).
[13] Youssef, interview; Messeh, interview; Hanna, interview.
[14] Messeh, interview (indicating how Bishop Moussa's books and sermons are available to North American churches as resources, but there is no direct guidance from the Bishopric); see, e.g., H.G. Bishop Moussa, *How to Speak to Youth* (Egypt: Bishopric of Youth, 2002); H.G. Bishop Moussa, *Youth Concerns (Question and Answer)* (Egypt: Bishopric of Youth, 2007).
[15] Youssef, interview.

effort for youth ministry in North America.[16]

As immigration in North America continued into new generations, youth ministry was not the top priority as the Coptic Church had many other dynamics to deal with such as immigrants adjusting to the culture and leaning on the Church for both financial and spiritual support. The first generation of immigrants was well educated, whereas the second generation of immigrants was not. As the generations grew, the cultural divide between the Egyptian born and the American-born widened. Clergy largely found themselves dealing with the unique dynamics of their congregation as well as various intrapersonal integration struggles within their flock's homes.[17]

As a result, over the years the Coptic parishes in North America did not develop a

---

[16] Ibid. (Bishop Youssef explained that the idea of Archdiocese involvement has begun by Fr. Luka Baselious Hermeina, within the Archdiocese in New Jersey, but still in a very early phase).

[17] Youssef, *Adapting to A New Place Called Home*, 71-82.

uniform approach to youth ministry, and most parishes mainly focused on creating a traditional Sunday school program with little attention made to comprehensive age-appropriate lesson plans or other aspects of youth ministry.[18] Web-based curriculum booklets, for example, are available for Coptic churches within the Southern Diocese at

---

[18] *See, e.g.*, Bishop Serapion, "Ninth Grade," *Sunday School Program of the Coptic Orthodox Church Diocese of Los Angeles, Southern California, and Hawaii* (August 27, 1999); Shenouda Anba Bishoy, *Topics for the Christian Youth*, (Illinois: St. Mark and St. Bishop Coptic Orthodox Church of Chicago, 1986); Coptic Orthodox Diocese of the Southern United States, "Sunday School Curriculum", https://www.suscopts.org/ssc/ (accessed March 12, 2018); Coptic Orthodox Church of Archangel Raphael and St. John the Beloved, "Sunday School Curriculum", http://www.chapelhillcoptic.net/dnn/en us/churchservices/curriculum.aspx (accessed March 12, 2018). The curriculum developed by the Southern Diocese and the Chapel Hill, North Carolina parish (respectively) provide a grade-by-grade breakdown of what a Sunday School teacher should cover for the class, but the individual lessons consist of the general overview of the topic and some discussion questions. None of the web-based programs offer comprehensive lesson-plans for a particular age group with designed activities or hands-on learning, but rather gives the volunteers the topics to teach week by week. The onus is still on the individual volunteer to develop a lesson plan around the designated topic.

https://www.suscopts.org/ssc/.[19]

The curriculum, however, only provides a grade-by-grade breakdown of what a Sunday school teacher should cover for the class. The responsibility is on the volunteer to create an age appropriate lesson plan with whatever particular activities, crafts, or discussion questions the individual volunteer deems necessary and can find on his or her own.[20] Bishop Youssef explained that it is up to the servant[21] to spend quiet time in prayer and allow the Holy Spirit to guide the content of the lesson so that they take ownership of their service and take their role seriously.[22] The drawback to this approach, however, is that the Sunday school curriculum is

---

[19] Coptic Orthodox Diocese of the Southern United States, "Sunday School Curriculum",
https://www.suscopts.org/ssc/ (accessed March 12, 2018).

[20] Ibid.; *see also* Youssef, interview.

[21] In the Coptic Church, the word "servant" is used to mean an unpaid volunteer who is a member of the Church. For purposes of this paper, the word "volunteer" is used interchangeably with "servant."

[22] Youssef, interview.

not regularly updated and the lesson quality differs from week to week entirely dependent on the volunteer who prepared the lesson.[23]

In more recent years, certain Coptic Orthodox parishes, dubbed "mission churches," have sprung up throughout North America with a focus on outreach to the American culture.[24] According to Fr. Anthony Messeh, a priest of one of these parishes in the Washington, D.C. area, St. Timothy and St. Athanasius (STSA), approximately 5-15 mission churches currently exist, but they are all very unique with differing approaches.[25] Fr. Anthony indicated the mission of STSA, for example, is "to bring an ancient faith to a modern world" with a focus on the community as a whole.[26] As far as youth ministry is concerned, STSA also does not pull curriculum

---

[23] Youssef, interview (discussing how although he is currently in the middle of updating the Southern Diocese curriculum, the material will again be outdated in a few years' time, and an ongoing solution is really what is needed).
[24] Messeh, interview.
[25] Ibid.
[26] Ibid.

from any universally available source, but rather relies on paid staff and volunteers to form the curriculum and the overall mission of youth ministry at STSA under his direction.[27] STSA also created various other programs to engage the youth in service in the community, service in the Church, and fellowship with one another.[28]

In general, however, STSA is the exception and not the rule. While Coptic parishes throughout North America are making an honest and passionate effort to try and reach the youth at their level, the focus is still on developing general Sunday school "curriculum"—that is, a manual of topics the parish (or in some cases, diocese) is expected to cover for each grade level. Most Coptic parishes, moreover, do not have paid or trained staff dedicated to youth ministry, but rather are completely volunteer run. Most Coptic

---

[27] Ibid. (Fr. Anthony recognized that using paid staff is generally not done in the Coptic Orthodox churches, but it is something STSA felt worth the investment).
[28] Messeh, interview.

parishes do not have a lot of resources or training to give to their volunteers and still face a lot of language and cultural barriers between the various generations within the congregation.[29]

In the context of how "young" the Coptic Orthodox Church is in North America, the amount of advances the Church has currently put forth into youth ministry is significant, to include increasing bishop and other clergy interest and involvement. Volunteers, moreover, tend to take their role very seriously and invest so much of themselves to the youth to become mentors and friends to the youth.[30] Bishop Youssef's diocese, in particular, heavily emphasizes "pre-servant" classes, which are required classes to become a

---

[29] Ibid.; Yousef, interview.
[30] Youssef, interview (describing the "Pre-Servants" classes implemented in his diocese, which starts in teenage years amongst youth identified as spiritually mature and future leaders. He explained they participate in Orthodox faith/theology classes with homework and exams for several years, followed by supervised volunteering, and finally leadership).

Sunday school teacher.[31] As Bishop Youssef explained, "you cannot be a doctor without graduating Medical School."[32] Bishop Moussa also developed a book made specifically on training volunteers on how to serve the youth.[33]

There is, however, much more work to do to heighten the standards and quality of youth ministry efforts in Coptic Orthodox parishes in North America. Where the focus has always been centered on Sunday school, youth ministry in North America ought to be more well-rounded diving into ways to help our youth connect to the Church and build their own identity and faith in God to raise up Orthodox young men and young women formed as children of God. Where each parish and/or diocese has created their own materials or otherwise put the burden on volunteers to create lesson plans, the Coptic Church ought to consider a larger body, perhaps

---

[31] Ibid.
[32] Ibid.
[33] Bishop Moussa, *How to Speak to Youth* (Bishopric of Youth, 2002).

a department of education, focused on creating and continually updating age-appropriate, theologically sound curriculum materials that any and all Coptic Orthodox parishes in North America could pull from and use in a parish youth ministry effort.

Overall, the passion, focus, and resources currently devoted into writing and re-writing Sunday school curriculum at parish or diocese levels should be steered into other mechanisms of youth ministry to best reach our youth and create a more well-rounded North American Coptic Orthodox youth ministry mission. Lesson planning, moreover, should not be a burden on a volunteer/servant, but rather delegated to a department of people who have the necessary qualifications, education, and passion to develop theologically sound, and developmentally age-appropriate materials. The Orthodox Church is one Body of Christ catering to the same mission: to aid our youth develop their own personal faith in Christ and continue that faith into the future generations of our Church. As outlined above, recent efforts suggest the Coptic Orthodox parishes in North America are facing a period of transition with regard to youth ministry.[34] Thus, this is the perfect time to decide what specifically the youth ministry blueprint should look like in the North American Coptic Orthodox parishes.

---

[34] Youssef, interview (noting efforts at the Archdiocese level recently began); Messeh, interview (noting differing approaches by "mission churches" throughout North America).

Sunday School Curriculum

As indicated above, there are two proposed main problems facing Coptic Orthodox parishes in North America today: (1). Framework and (2). Curriculum. This book is largely focused on framework. With regard to curriculum, several papers could be written just about this topic. What is proposed here is that youth ministry is more than a Sunday school curriculum. Curriculum is not "magic," is not the "solution," and is certainly not a replacement for youth ministry. A mind shift is necessary in the Coptic Orthodox Church to view curriculum as merely one of many tools that can be used by a parish in a youth ministry effort.

However, there is no doubt a growing need in the Coptic Orthodox Church for a consistent source that individual North American parishes can pull resources from to aid in the creation of their youth ministry effort. The consistent source must be theologically sound, but also age-appropriate from a social, cognitive, and educational perspective. As recognized by the Coptic Bishop of Youth, Bishop Moussa, speaking to youth requires reaching them on multiple dimensions: spiritual, biblical, ecclesiastic, scientific, practical, and missionary.[35]

Accomplishing such a curriculum effectively and consistently requires lesson plans created by a team of experts ensuring that materials have a cohesive flow from one week to the next, are age appropriate, are theologically sound, and are regularly updated. In other words, to truly be an effective tool for parishes to use,

---

[35] Moussa, *How to Speak to Youth*.

curriculum writing should be delegated away from volunteers and towards a proper specialized team. Resources would then be made available to the parishes at large to pull from and adapt to fit their individual youth ministry effort.

Such a need has been satisfied in other churches by a Department of Education, with a diverse staff of people with degrees in theology, psychology, education, and human development.[36] The Coptic Orthodox Church must consider developing a similar effort in North America to fully solve the "curriculum problem." Indeed, the idea of a universally available curriculum is not new in the Coptic Orthodox Church. Indeed, the establishment of the "Sunday School movement" in the Coptic Orthodox Church

---

[36] *See, e.g.*, Antiochian Orthodox Christian Archdiocese of North America, "The Department of Christian Education," http://ww1.antiochian.org/christianeducation (accessed September 10, 2018); Greek Orthodox Archdiocese of America, "Department of Religious Education," https://www.goarch.org/departments/religioused (accessed September 10, 2018).

occurred in the mid-nineteenth century in large part as a response to Western missions in Egypt.[37] The American Presbyterian and Catholic movements in Egypt had set up religious education activity, which no doubt inspired the work of archdeacon St. Habib Girgis.[38] St. Habib Girgis felt that education was the best weapon to protect the youth from conversion away from the Church and he created a universally available Sunday school curriculum available to all Orthodox parishes in Egypt to use.[39]

For illustration purposes, Sunday school lesson plans can be found in the appendices of this book.[40] These lesson plans highlight an effective way to reach the North American youth of the Coptic Orthodox parishes that are age appropriate and theologically sound.

Appendix I, for example, provides the

---

[37] Suriel, *Habib Girgis*, 61.
[38] Ibid., 61-63.
[39] Ibid., Ch. 3.
[40] The lesson plans found in appendices I-IV are excerpts from the author's published curriculum units available at http://www.bridgestoorthodoxy.com.

lesson plan of the Old Testament story of Joseph and how he trusted God no matter what, catered for an elementary-aged class.[41] The lesson plan is focused on the fruits of the spirit "goodness" and "faithfulness" and shows how even when bad things happened to Joseph, he had faith that God is a good God and things would work for good in the end. Joseph had trust in God even though it seemed like he was getting punished for making good choices! The premise of the lesson is to encourage the elementary-aged youth that even if sometimes they "miss out" on something fun because they are saying no to a bad choice, God will reward their faithfulness and trust in Him. The lesson plan incorporates crafts, activities that get the children moving, and age-appropriate discussion questions. Such aspects are pillars of keeping a lesson plan effective and engaging to an elementary-aged child.[42]

---

[41] *See* Appendix I.
[42] Koulomzin, *Our Church and Our Children*, 57 (indicating, "the key theme of moral education through middle childhood is the development of the child's realization and

Appendix II provides the same Old Testament lesson of Joseph but catered to teens.[43] The lesson plan highlighted here is one of the weeks (week 3) of a month long Bible-study into the nuances of trusting in God and why when we put our trust in other people, things, even ourselves, we are let down. The teens are challenged to think through why we are tempted to put our trust in other things sometimes and how those things (even family or our best friends) let us down sometimes and why our only true hope is to abide in the love of God; to Him we are never forgotten. The lesson plan incorporates an opening game, a video clip, age-appropriate discussion questions, and an application activity for teens to consider these hard questions. Such a lesson plan is catered for adolescent characteristics of "sensitivity" and "dissatisfaction," by addressing how their

---

appreciation of the relations that link him to other people and to God.").

[43] *See* Appendix II.

everyday lives are never forgotten to God—that they matter to God.[44] Both lessons tie the message to a tangible application for them to appreciate how the well-known Bible story relates to their daily lives. Appendix III, moreover, is a lesson-plan from a unit on the Seven Sacraments, designed for a 5th-6th grade classroom ("preteens") catered to teaching the age group specifically about communion.[45] In Appendix IV, another example is provided of an Orthodox-Faith topic lesson-plan from a unit explaining where the Orthodox Creed came from and the details of the Ecumenical Councils.[46] It is no easy task taking concepts such as the Sacraments, Ecumenical Councils, and the Orthodox Creed and converting them into age-appropriate lesson-plans that will engage and benefit the youth. Appendix III and IV are attached to further

---

[44] Koulomzin, *Our Church and Our Children*, 70-71 (talking about how adolescents are generally sensitive and dissatisfied with themselves, their family, etc. as they seek identity and acceptance).
[45] *See* Appendix III.
[46] *See* Appendix IV.

illustrate the need of a department of specifically trained educators that can create both theologically sound materials and materials that will resonate with the youth age groups.

Rather than putting the onus on the volunteers to create lesson plans week to week, it is crucial that Coptic parishes begin to recognize that lesson planning is something that requires a certain level of education and expertise. While it is crucial that volunteers take their responsibility seriously, the focus of their responsibility should be shifted away from lesson planning towards forming strong bonds with the youth. Youth crave good, adult role-models, and Coptic parishes have a responsibility to equip their volunteers to succeed.[47] Rather than individual parishes or diocese writing and re-writing curriculum, the Coptic Orthodox parishes of North America should strive to come together as one body and form an educated and

---

[47] *See* Part III, "ENGAGE VOLUNTEERS," *supra*. (discussing the role of the volunteer).

specialized department devoted to creating theologically sound and age-appropriate resources for the Church as a whole.

Proposed Framework for Youth Ministry

With curriculum delegated to a larger body, individual parishes in North America will be free to use such resources in reshaping and refocusing the goals and vision of any youth ministry effort. The youth need the parish to be there for them. Youth are under an overwhelming amount of pressure to be conformed to this world. The main-stream media is constantly telling youth what should be important to them, what they should think, what is desirable, and what is not desirable.[48] Unfortunately, many of these ideas are contrary to Orthodox teachings and rob them of personhood, standing in the way of them becoming sons and daughters of God.[49] Kids have a great desire to be liked and will face the challenge daily to stay true to who they are in Christ in the face of this contradiction.

A common myth is that church-attending youth are somehow different or "better" than their peers—as if they are the "good youth" and non-church goers are automatically the "bad kids."[50] It is a dangerous myth because it seems to minimize the importance of vision in a youth ministry, as if it doesn't matter the approach because the Church is already ministering to "good" kids. The truth is, regardless of the specific congregation, a youth ministry effort will face some of the same challenges. In Erikson's book

---

[48] *See e.g.*, Stanley S. Harakas, *Living the Faith: The Praxis of Eastern Orthodox Ethics* (Minnesota: Light and Life Publishing Company, 1982), 226-227.
[49] Ibid.
[50] Merton P. Strommen, *Five Cries of Youth* (San Francisco: Harper & Row, 1979), 8-9.

Identity Youth and Crisis, the general struggles people deal with growing from infancy to adulthood are the same regardless of religion, ethnicity, or race. Most significantly, identity confusion—who are they and how do they fit into the story of salvation? Erikson describes an identity confusion that occurs during adolescence where youth want to find their identity in something—a career path, a certain group of friends, a sport, a faith—but at the same time are cynically mistrusting of being identified with something.[51] Accordingly, for a youth ministry effort to be successful, the goal must be in

---

[51] Erik H. Erikson, *Identity Youth and Crisis* (New York: W.W. Norton & Company, 1994), 128-135; *see also* Joseph F. Purpura, *Moral and Ethical Issues: Confronting Orthodox Christian Teens Across North America* (1st Books Library, 2002), 56. In Purpura's book and preparation of survey results, he indicates teens identified with the following top concerns: grades, being liked, fears, and getting along with parents. "Many teens have expressed that what really matters is that they get a good education so they can make a lot of money and therefore be successful. I rarely hear a teen saying they want to get a good education so they can live a fuller and more meaningful life. Purpura, *Moral and Ethical Issues*, 56.

assisting youth find their own faith and identity in God rather than merely teaching stories or forcing a theology on them.[52]

Before proposing any changes to the format of youth ministry, it is important to first spend some time discussing and, in fact, precisely defining what is the purpose or the mission behind creating a youth ministry in the Coptic Orthodox Church.[53] Without a clear vision, youth programs tend to just fill needs (like childcare) rather than provide a meaningful and spiritual mission. A youth ministry effort in a parish is not merely an effort to create a fellowship group, but aimed to form young people in the image of God—it has importance beyond the vision of

---

[52] Sophie Koulomzin, *Our Church and Our Children* (Yonkers: St. Vladimir's Seminary Press, 2004), Ch. 1.
[53] Douglas Fields, *Purpose Driven Youth Ministry: 9 Essential Foundations for Healthy Growth*, (Michigan: Zondervan, 1998), 34-39, 43, 55-80 (indicating that before haphazardly starting a youth program, Church leaders should take a step back and articulate the "why" – what is the purpose behind creating a Youth Ministry).

other youth programs, such as Girl/Boy Scouts. Many times, programs put together without a plan or vision, lack any kind of organization or preparation and participating volunteers leave feeling frustrated and that their time was wasted.[54] By creating *and articulating* the youth ministry vision, volunteers will also be encouraged to become a part of that vision and bring "quality" to the vision.[55] Having a clearly articulated purpose statement for the youth ministry will clarify the ministry, attract followers, minimize conflicts, build excitement, and add professionalism to the youth ministry effort.[56] Ultimately, spiritually led youth ministry leaders should take the time to pray through and clearly articulate what the vision of the Church's youth ministry effort will be so that any

---

[54] *See* Bill Hybels, *The Volunteer Revolution: Unleashing the Power of Everybody* (Michigan: Zondervan, 2004), 25; *see also* Tony Morgan and Tim Stevens, *Simply Strategic Volunteers: Empowering People for Ministry* (Colorado: Group, 2005), 89-90 (talking about respecting volunteers' time).
[55] Morgan and Stevens, *Simply Strategic Volunteers*, 73-74.
[56] Fields, *Purpose Driven Youth Ministry*, 56-60.

participant—be a leader, volunteer, student, parent, or clergy—can get excited about it and actively participate in this mission plan.

In the Orthodox Church, the overarching purpose behind youth ministry must be to make the Orthodox Christian faith real and personal to every youth so that they are still in the Church when they reach adulthood and continue to thrive in their faith throughout adulthood.[57] Indeed, the incarnation of Jesus Christ and the inevitable incarnational nature of the Church is the means by which we, humans, can be made god.[58] Said another way, youth ministry should help young people integrate "fully into the total life of the Church."[59]

---

[57] *See generally* Thomas Joseph, "Youth Formation," symposium, https://teensoyo.org/youth-formation/ (accessed August 17, 2018); Joseph F. Purpura, "Youth Formation," symposium, https://teensoyo.org/youth formation (accessed August 17, 2018).

[58] Sorial, *Incarnational Exodus*, 21 (discussing St. Athanasius explanation of the importance of the link between of the incarnation of Christ and the incarnational nature of the Church, asserting, "God became human that we might be made god.").

[59] Purpura, *Moral and Ethical Issues*, 24.

Christian morality is not merely about obedience, but rather the ultimate goal is eternal life, "blessed and joyful sharing in the life of the triune God."[60] Most of what youth learn in Sunday school will be forgotten if the Church does not also help them develop a sense of deep abiding self-worth in God. Godly importance must trump worldly importance. Godly acceptance must become more important than being "liked" or being "popular." According to Antiochian Orthodox Bishop Thomas, the mission of youth ministry is helping young minds form their own personal faith so as they mature they are able to maneuver such moral and ethical issues relying on God.[61] When they become adults, the hope is that they feel belonging and ownership with the Orthodox Church and faith and that they rely on God to reveal their talents, gifts, and passions to share with the Church community.

---

[60] John Breck, *The Sacred Gift of Life*, (Yonkers: St. Vladimir's Seminary Press, 2000), 23.
[61] Joseph, "Youth Formation."

As proposed in Koulomzin's book, *Our Church and Our Children*, there are 5 main prongs in Christian faith development in a child's mind. First, the child must develop a "sense of the reality of God." That is, the child must understand that God is not merely a character in a book, but a real and living entity that we can interact with on a regular basis.[62] A child should discover his or her belonging in the Body of Christ; that the Church is their home as much as it is the adults.[63] Sr. Magdalen, in her book, *Children in the Church Today*, also notes how the Orthodox Church is distinct from Protestant churches in that we do not have a "children's church." Children are full members of the Body of the Christ and, therefore, the Orthodox Church does not deprive kids of the experience of the Liturgy.[64] A child should grow in spiritual knowledge and technical

---

[62] Sophie Koulomzin, *Our Church and Our Children* (New York: St. Vladimir's Seminary Press, 2004), 19-23.
[63] Koulomzin, *Our Church and Our Children*, 23-24.
[64] Sr. Magdalen, *Children in the Church Today: An Orthodox Perspective* (New York: St. Vladimir's Seminary Press, 1991), 59.

understanding of the Orthodox faith through religious education (i.e., Sunday school).[65]

Youth should also come to understand and appreciate the Holy Mystery, the "Fear of God." Koulomzin eloquently describes this as "children's sense of awe" cultivated "to help them recognize God's action within the realm of their experience of life."[66] In the context of youth ministry, the Church should offer mentorship and discipleship opportunities for youth to spiritually grow and develop this ability to recognize God's action in their lives.

Finally, youth ministry should offer "Wholeness" in religious education because Christianity is not a compartment; it is not something they are only on Sundays, but something that is who they are in all parts of the world they live in.[67] Maturing adolescents should be given opportunities to discover his or her

---

[65] Koulomzin, *Our Church and Our Children*, 24-26.
[66] Ibid., 27.
[67] Ibid., 29-31.

unique talents and passions and use them to serve in some capacity. Youth should feel encouraged to discover who God made them to be and to integrate that into all aspects of their life, not just their "spiritual life" on Sundays. In the youth ministry context, it may include visiting other parishes, visiting monastic communities, and overall feeling encouraged to contribute to serve in Church is some capacity.[68]

Clearly, there are many facets to adolescent development, and youth ministry should go beyond a traditional Sunday school program. Indeed, the traditional Sunday school program merely fulfills only one of the five prongs discussed by Koulomzin.

Koulomzin's five-prong approach to youth ministry (hereinafter referred to "Koulomzin's Five Prongs") neatly fit into a mission statement for youth ministry in the Coptic Orthodox Church and should be at the forefront for any format

---

[68] Sr. Magdalen, *Children in the Church Today*, 69.

undertaking. Whatever program, retreat, outing, or service a parish does should be for the purpose of fulfilling one or more of these five- prongs: "Sense of Reality of God"; "One Body of God"; "Religious Education"; "Holy Mystery/Fear of God"; and "Wholeness." In essence – the mission statement for youth ministry in the Coptic Orthodox Church ought to be: for youth to know that God is real and living; to develop a personal faith and personal sense of "awe" seeing God work in their lives; to have religious knowledge of their faith; to know that they are fully part of the Body of Christ with unique talents and gifts given to them by the Holy Spirit; and to discover and use those gifts for the fulfillment of Christ's purpose because they are not merely Christians on Sunday, but it is their whole self.

    Fulfilling the mission will require not just a closer examination of the traditional Sunday school program, but also a look at how youth are engaged during the Sunday Liturgy and what meaningful outside-Sunday programs are necessary to further develop a well-rounded youth ministry effort. With Koulomzin's five-prongs at the forefront, any and all changes to youth ministry require the following next steps: (1) understand the audience ("Wholeness" Prong): linking youth ministry to the practical lives of the youth; (2) hire paid staff (Holy Mystery "Fear of God" Prong): allocating resources for paid youth ministry staff; (3) engage volunteers ("Reality of God" Prong): selecting and equipping volunteers for success; (4) create meaningful programs ("Body of Christ" Prong): helping youth discover their unique place in the Body of Christ; (5) connect with families ("Religious Education" Prong): partnering with parents; and (6) stay current (fosters all of Koulomzin's five prongs): ongoing efforts to understand current youth needs.[69]

---

[69] *See also* Appendix V (a chart summary of all proposed changes discussed herein).

Wholeness: Bridging Ministry and Practicality

Any youth ministry program, even if designed with Koulomzin's five prongs specifically in mind, will only be effective as they are designed specifically with the youth audience in mind and in their "language." For example, teaching the concept of Koulomzin's "reality of God" prong will be a completely different endeavor with a five year old than with a fifteen-year old. Koulomzin proposes, for example, that a five-year old may first need basic understanding that God is not merely a character in his or her storybook, but a real, living being capable of being experienced.[70] Indeed, this is one of many reasons why children are encouraged to be part of Liturgical worship.[71] A fifteen-year old, on the other hand, may need opportunities to have deep and meaningful

---

[70] Koulomzin, *Our Church and Our Children*, 19-23.
[71] Sr. Magdalen, *Children in the Church Today*, 59.

experiences with the living God, such as mentorship relationships, participation in the Liturgical services, and/or spiritual retreats.[72]

Younger children have short attention spans and require different types of learning: activities, games, arts and crafts, etc.[73] Preschool and elementary-aged kids need to be told how Biblical principles and virtues are important to their daily lives. Again, relating back to Koulomzin's five prongs, the idea is to help youth understand the wholeness of their faith—that they are not just Christians on Sunday, but that the Biblical principles and virtues they learn on Sunday apply to their everyday life.[74] Children need an element of "fun" to keep their attention with age appropriate lessons. Overall, younger preschool and elementary-aged children need

---

[72] See also Appendices I - IV for examples of lesson plans catered for elementary-aged kids (Appendices I and III) and the same lesson catered for teens (Appendices II and IV).
[73] Koulomzin, *Our Church and Our Children*, Ch. 4 (discussing general teaching methods for various ages); John L. Boojamra, *Foundations for Christian Education* (Yonkers: St. Vladimir's Seminary Press, 1989).
[74] Koulomzin, *Our Church and Our Children*, 29-31.

"childish amusement," a place to let off steam and freedom from responsibilities.[75]

Once a child reaches adolescents and teenage years, however, their needs radically change and it is important that youth ministry understands and responds accordingly. The youth quickly and loudly become bombarded with images and messages related to dating, sexuality, pornography, alcohol, drugs, social media, and many other tough social, moral, and ethical issues. The idea of preserving ones "purity" is largely antiquated in much of our American, secular culture, it is often deemed old fashioned and perhaps unrealistic by many and thus has become one of the most critical issues facing today's Orthodox Christian youth. It is important to address this issue with our youth as early as possible/appropriate while the questions are still theoretical. Once emotions become involved, it is harder to reach our

---

[75] Sr. Magdalen, *Children in the Church Today*, 71-74.

Orthodox youth and direct them on a correct path. A youth ministry program that does not seek to understand the landscape of which our teens are trying to maneuver does a big disservice to the ministry of these young minds.[76]

The underlying foundation for all moral and ethical issues confronting our youth today is an overwhelming amount of pressure to be conformed to this world. In combating this pressure, youth ministry should address critical moral and ethical issues and equip our young people to live a healthy spiritual life in this fallen world.[77] The cultural agenda, which is focused on immediate pleasure and experimentation, is in stark contrast to the never-changing Church, which stresses a deification process that leads to eternal life.[78]

---

[76] Stanley S. Harakas, *Contemporary Moral Issues* (Minnesota: Light and Life Publishing, 1982), 75 (indicating it is the Church's responsibility to help develop our children's "wholesome Christian attitude" towards sex and the family unit)].
[77] Harakas, *Living the Faith*, 86-87.
[78] See Breck, *The Sacred Gift of Life*, 56-58.

Textbooks and curriculum have their value, but they will not in and of themselves teach the youth how to be good Orthodox Christian.[79] While the content of the lesson is important, understanding this audience means understanding adolescents' absolute need for strong bonds with people they can look up to and trust. The first sign of a Christian community is love for all. Youth need to come to learn discernment and understand that everyone, except Christ, is imperfect living in an imperfect world and everyone is in need of compassion, forgiveness and love. Effective youth ministry stretches beyond pure facts and knowledge of a biblical curriculum. Volunteers should be motivated to share and encourage personal faith.[80] Influencing the youth should be through mutual respect and building a relationship with them, being available, showing interest, and

---

[79] Koulomzin, *Our Church and Our Children*, 13.
[80] Strommen, *Five Cries of Youth*, 4-9 (also describing the challenge of developing this bond as almost a different language).

communicating with them.[81]

Indeed, once youth reach middle-school years, they desperately long for a place they belong, an environment where they feel safe and loved.[82] If the Church provides a place for the youth to fill this need, then it can help teens resist the temptation filling this need in more destructive places. It is not that the Orthodox Church should create a bubble of isolation around our youth, but to understand the needs of the audience. Youth need to live in this world, but live as Christians—as children of God.

If a parish's youth ministry neglects to instruct and indeed model behavior of choosing God's affections over the world's affections, the program fails to truly understand its audience.

> "We want our young people to find strength and courage in the teachings of our Lord rather than feeling embarrassed or feeling

---

[81] Ibid., 118-121.
[82] Orthodox Church in America, "A Vision on Youth Ministry," *The Hub*, https://oca.org/the-hub/about youth-ministry/a-vision-on-youth-ministry (accessed Sept. 11, 2018).

strange about sharing what they believe.... We want our teens to find strength in being different from this fallen world...."[83]

By creating a safe environment for them with positive adult role models, adults willing to spend time with them, and like-minded youth, our young people will have an environment where they will always belong and where they always have friends.[84]

In short, it is imperative that any youth ministry effort understands its audience. For younger preschool or elementary-aged kids, content needs to be delivered in a way for children to understand how it applies to their "whole" self. Instructors must understand the short attention span and the need for kids this age to learn through multiple activities, games,

---

[83] Purpura, *Moral and Ethical Issues,* 25-26; see also Mark 8:38 (NKJV), "For whoever is ashamed of me and of my words in this adulterous and sinful generation, of him will the Son of man also be ashamed, when he comes in the glory of His father with the holy angels."

[84] See generally Purpura, *Moral and Ethical Issues,* 83; see also Harakas, *Living the Faith,* 172-174.

and arts and crafts. For adolescents and teens, any youth ministry effort must address ethical and moral issues because these are their current struggles that stand in the way of their relationship with Christ and His Church. These students need a place to develop a firm foundation in Christ, a personal relationship with God, and correct direction with positive role models.

Working together with parents, the youth ministry has a unique opportunity to help shape the moral compass of our young congregation members. It is the entire Church's responsibility to help our children develop a "wholesome Christian attitude" with regard to these critical ethical and moral issues.[85] The goal of youth ministry is not merely to persuade youth to live an Orthodox set of moral and ethical values, as though the Church simply preserves cultural norms, but rather to foster an environment where

---

[85] Harakas, *Contemporary Moral Issues*, 75.

they choose to fervently seek to live their life as a child of God.

Fear of God: Allocating Resources for Paid Youth Ministry

Koulomzin's "Fear of God" prong indicates that an element of youth ministry must be devoted to helping youth come to understand and appreciate the Holy Mystery of God and recognize God's action in the realm of their experience of life.[86] Parishes should never allow youth ministry to replace the Divine Liturgy, but rather help and equip youth to fully participate in the Liturgy.[87] To that end, youth ministry requires an element of mentorship and discipleship. Whether it be instructing boys on the altar or youth in a Church choir, or encouraging and instructing youth through their first time confessing, much of this prong requires youth to be exposed to good, spiritual role

---

[86] Koulomzin, *Our Church and Our Children*, 27.
[87] Koulomzin, *Our Church and Our Children*, 12-13.

models.

In the Coptic Orthodox parishes in North America, helping youth with Liturgical engagement is not typically accomplished by any prescribed method or program, but on an *ad hoc* basis by deacons or other laity. That is, in most Coptic Orthodox parishes in North America today, youth ministry is solely volunteer-run.[88] It is very rare that you will find a parish that has employed a leader in a paid position outside of clergy, and even more rare in youth ministry specifically.[89]

Unfortunately, when a parish utilizes solely a volunteer-run program, the parish necessarily limits the focus of youth ministry to one main facet of learning (typically Sunday school).[90] Volunteers, who take their role seriously but nonetheless do not typically have

---

[88] Messeh, interview; Hanna, interview; Youssef, interview; Hanna, interview.
[89] Ibid.
[90] Again, in many Coptic Churches the word "servant" is used to mean a volunteer and, therefore, for purposes of this paper, the words "servant" and "volunteer" are used interchangeably.

theological degrees or advanced training in youth ministry, shoulder the responsibility of every aspect of a parish's youth ministry effort along with their full-time jobs and familial responsibilities. Bishop Youssef described the types of training of volunteers in a Coptic Church that is typical, called "pre-servants classes," that prepare volunteers to teach Sunday School and serve in a mentorship and discipleship role.[91] He explained that starting with teenagers, future leaders are identified and they go through several years of training and religious education to prepare them to be an adult-servant.[92] While certainly comprehensive, this process clearly has drawbacks. The focus, for one, is limited to teaching volunteers theologically-correct information so that they can be good Sunday school teachers.[93] Ongoing turnover and, of course, finding people willing to make such a time

---

[91] Youssef, interview.
[92] Ibid.
[93] Youssef, interview.

commitment on a volunteer basis are other drawbacks of such an approach.

In short, a volunteer-run youth ministry effort will always be limited because resources, education, and volunteers' time will always be limited.

In contrast, many Eastern Orthodox Churches and Protestant Churches will have a combination of paid staff fully devoted to youth ministry supported by volunteers. The leader or paid staff members, moreover, have theological degrees and formal training in youth ministry whereas the expectations of the volunteers are different. It is proposed that this scenario, the combination of leader/paid-staff and volunteers, is more ideal than a completely volunteer-run youth ministry effort. A full-time paid staff member will be able to focus time and energy in a way that volunteers will rarely be able to do.

If parishes seek to hire at least one paid staff member ("leader") devoted to youth ministry, the scope of the ministry can broaden.

More attention can be made to other aspects of the Orthodox faith, such as Liturgical engagement, discipleship, and mentorship. The (paid) leader, with the priest, should be in charge of setting the vision of the youth ministry effort, selecting and training volunteers, properly equipping and supporting these volunteer servants for success, and constantly shaping the youth ministry effort by adding ministries or dimensions to fit the needs of the particular parish. Volunteers, in turn, have responsibilities as well and ought to share in the vision, but should not be required to shoulder the same kind of responsibilities.

Fr. Anthony Messeh, the Coptic Orthodox priest of a "mission focused" parish in North America, indicated that he employed a Director of Youth Ministry because "when something is important, you should invest in it."[94] Clearly

---

[94] Messeh, interview; see also Hanna, interview (indicating his church does not currently have paid staff-members, but he feels it is worth the investment in the future because

acknowledging being the exception and not the rule for most Coptic Orthodox parishes in North America, he feels that you do not have to be a priest to be devoted to and qualified for youth ministry. His parish's children's program is "one of the most important facets of the Church" and, therefore he wanted to invest in it by hiring a paid director.[95] "If adults like church, but their kids do not—they will not come back. And we've seen the reverse. Kids are bringing their parents back."[96]

This approach, however, should be done carefully and deliberately. Parishes should make the selection of the paid leader carefully. He or she should have an authentic and sincere faith, a theological degree and/or youth ministry training, a natural ability to communicate with children, and the capacity to grow and develop gifts.[97]

"you are sending a message to the congregation that this ministry is of high importance.").
[95] Messeh, interview.
[96] Ibid.
[97] Koulomzin, *Our Church and Our Children*, 18 and Ch. 5.

Parishes should also regularly evaluate whether the leader is a good match for the position, and have a mechanism to allow for leaders to leave and/or for parishes to end the employment without devastation of the spiritual life of the leader.

Parishes should also be wary of youth ministry developing into a staff "job." Orthodox youth ministry must focus first and foremost on spirituality.[98] Havrilak writes, "youth ministry is the fellowship with Christ realized in life."[99] So, on the one hand, if youth ministry develops merely into a "job," the focus becomes action oriented rather than faith oriented. The "doing" is less important than helping youth experience spirituality and demonstrating that through adult role models.[100] The goal is formation—forming young people.

---

[98] Gregory Havrilak, "Youth Ministry: A Foundation," Orthodox Church in America, https://oca.org/the hub/leader-info-about-youth-ministry/youth-ministry-a foundation1 (accessed Sept. 10, 2018).
[99] Ibid.
[100] Ibid.

Thus, to that extent, the role of a paid leader will have some similarities to the role of a volunteer/servant. Both should be expected to first and foremost focus on their own walk with God, seeking His will through prayer, and placing trust in God that our efforts will produce His will. In fact, a self-check to ensure spiritual-only motivation is needed for both leaders and volunteers on a regular basis.[101] Leaders and volunteers alike should also be of the mindset that at the end of the day they are not serving their own egos, parents, clergy, or even the kids directly, but rather we are living sacrifices to the Lord.[102]

Both leaders and volunteers should be selected based not only on spiritual maturity, but also on a natural ability to communicate with

---

[101] Hybels, *The Volunteer Revolution*, 132; see also Fields, *Purpose Driven Youth Ministry*, 28-29 (explaining that without spiritual leaders, any youth ministry effort will be essentially empty on the inside).

[102] See Morgan and Stevens, *Simply Strategic Volunteers*, 73-74 (recounts how leaders and volunteers need to be constantly on guard/in check about their motives; their ministry should never be about themselves).

children.[103] Sister Magdalen says, "The most valuable teachers are those who have a good relationship with the children."[104] A successful youth ministry effort will require good, healthy, and spiritual relationships between spiritually led role-models and the youth. Aside from selecting the leader and volunteers carefully, parishes should allow for some freedom for leaders and volunteers to leave the ministry when it becomes obvious that it is not a good match.

In other crucial aspects, however, the role of a leader is much different than the role of a volunteer. It is the paid leader, along with the parish priest, however, who will make or break the ministry and set the tone of the program— good or bad. Without an effective leader, moreover, a parish will always suffer from eventual burn out of volunteers, who are tasked

---

[103] Hybels, *The Volunteer Revolution*, 81-82; Morgan and Stevens, *Simply Strategic Volunteers*, 41-42; see also Fields, *Purpose Driven Youth Ministry*, Chapters 15 and 16.
[104] Sr. Magdalen, *Children in the Church Today*, 51.

with full-time jobs to do in their spare time.[105] Leaders should also be empowered to select, train, and properly equip volunteers ("servants"). The role of the volunteer is fleshed out more in the next section. For purposes of this prong, however, the success of the volunteer will ultimately be led by the efforts of the paid-staff leader. Thus, a leader should be one who understands the volunteers' role. Leaders should be able to motivate and encourage volunteers to bless the program with their own unique talents and style. A leader is someone who will understand that youth ministry is not merely babysitting kids or in charge of "crowd control," but rather an important responsibility to minister and disciple the students as they grow in their faith and learn to connect to God personally.[106]

In short, Koulomzin's "Fear of God" prong

---

[105] Fields, *Purpose Driven Youth Ministry*, 271; Hybels, *The Volunteer Revolution*, 25.
[106] Fields, *Purpose Driven Youth Ministry*, 272.

is a crucial element in youth ministry within the Orthodox Church because of the Sacramental nature of the Orthodox faith. It is through the Church, through Liturgical worship, through participation in the Sacraments, that the youth will come to understand and appreciate the Holy Mysteries of God.[107] In any youth ministry effort parishes should be emphasizing theological teachings (i.e., the Bible, the Liturgies, prayers, hymns, canons, saints, writings of the Fathers, etc.) *and* personal relationship with Christ.[108] For too long, Coptic Orthodox parishes relied solely on volunteer-run youth programs that fall short in terms of mentorship, discipleship, and scope. Investing in at least on paid staff member devoted to youth ministry will go a long way to fill this gap. A paid leader, especially one with

---

[107] Ibid., 27.
[108] Pearl Gaskins, *I Believe In....: Christian, Jewish, and Muslim Young People Speak About Their Faith* (Chicago: Cricket Books, 2004) (showing numerous stories by youth telling similar stories of searching for identity, connection to their place of worship, and wanting for religion to be beyond a mere cultural distinction).

education and spiritual maturity, will be uniquely focused on casting the vision for youth ministry, creating meaningful programs, and ensuring volunteers are properly selected, trained, and equipped for success.

Reality of God: Selecting and Equipping Volunteers for Success

The "Reality of God" prong of youth ministry, as proposed by Koulomzin, is aimed at helping the youth understand and giving them opportunities to experience God—not merely as a character in a book, but as the living God.[109] This prong will play out in various ways in youth ministry depending on the age groups and depending on the size of the church. Preschool curriculum, teen retreats, quiet time challenges, prayer meetings, etc., are examples of ways youth ministry can give youth the opportunities to experience the living God for themselves.

---

[109] Koulomzin, *Our Church and Our Children*, 19-23.

Before implementing any program, however, it is imperative that a church thinks through not only who will be the leader(s), but how those leaders will choose and equip volunteers (servants) for success. Programs may be designed to help kids discover the "Reality of God," but without a successful team of leaders and volunteers who are genuine role models, the programs will be essentially empty inside.[110]

As discussed in the prior section, each individual parish ought to have at least one paid youth ministry staff member (i.e., "leader") that, among other things, will be empowered to select and equip volunteers, with the blessing of the parish priest.

Ideally, spiritually mature volunteers, with a gift for working with youth, should be selected and properly motivated to demonstrate and

---

[110] Hybels, *The Volunteer Revolution*, 132; see also Fields, *Purpose Driven Youth Ministry*, 28-29.

encourage a personal faith in Christ.[111] This is, however, no easy task as many parishes struggle with the same problem: not enough committed volunteers. It becomes tempting as a leader to fill empty slots with adult "supervisors" rather than spirit-led role models.

There is no doubt, however, that regardless of the lack, a successful youth ministry depends on picking volunteers who will take their responsibility seriously.[112] Adolescents crave adult role models and advocates.[113] In a study conducted amongst youth who were especially gifted or inspired, there was one common trend when asked the source of their inspiration—they all point to a teacher.[114]

---

[111] Strommen, *Five Cries of Youth*, 9 (pointing out statistical data that such a personal relationship with God made a huge impact in the lifestyle of the teen).

[112] Sophie Koulomzin, "Children and Christian Education," Orthodox Church in America, https://oca.org/the-hub/leader-info-about-youth-ministry/children-and-christian-education1 (accessed Sept. 10, 2018).

[113] Erikson, *Identity: Youth and Crisis*, 135-141 (discussing youth's need for intimacy and feeling that they are "somebody").

[114] Erikson, *Identity: Youth and Crisis*, 125.

Finding and properly equipping the right volunteers for youth ministry is so vitally important that numerous books have been written just about this specific topic![115]

There always seems to be some amount of guilt asking volunteers for their time, much less putting "burdensome" expectations on them, but as any seasoned servant will tell you, it is a bigger blessing to the participant than to the Church.[116] God will always fill the needs of His Church, but the joy that comes from volunteering in the Church is something a person earns from sincerity of heart.

Selecting Volunteers

An ideal volunteer (servant) in a parish youth ministry program should be spiritually led,

---

[115] See *e.g.,* Fields, *Purpose Driven Youth Ministry*, Ch. 15- 19; Morgan and Stevens, *Simply Strategic Volunteers*; Hybels, *The Volunteer Revolution.*

[116] See Hybels, *The Volunteer Revolution,* 11-12 (the author encourages Churches to never feel guilty asking members to volunteer because volunteering in a Church ministry bring meaning to our souls, it delights our Father, and brings immense joy to the participant).

committed, and genuinely gifted in working with youth.[117]

Volunteers should not even be considered for youth ministry service if they are not nourishing their own spiritual life or participating fully in the Sacramental life of the Church. Character is of upmost importance-- ideally volunteers in a youth ministry effort will be devout Orthodox Christians, responsible, full of integrity, and full of passion for the youth ministry vision. Volunteers must have an authentic faith of their own and be willing to share it with youth. It is also important that volunteers have the ability to communicate with kids at their level or be willing to learn to be a relevant friend to the youth. Said another way, volunteers need to be a good combination of fun loving *and* spiritual. Youth do not need "programs," they need reliable, Orthodox relationships with faith filled adults who actually

---

[117] Koulomzin, *Our Church and Our Children*, 18 and Ch. 5.

live out their lives as they preach.[118] It should be emphasized, however, that volunteers should not be expected to be free from sin.[119] Rather, it is important that volunteers within the youth ministry programs are spiritually mature, striving towards deification and actively participating in the Sacraments of the Church. Part of being spiritually mature is also expecting volunteers to obey their spiritual leaders and serve with a sense of humility.[120] That is not to say that volunteers cannot take ownership of their service; indeed, they must take ownership or they will not flourish in the ministry. Taking ownership, however, is different than leadership, and spiritually mature volunteers should ultimately understand that they are all merely stewards of God's children, instruments for His

---

[118] Michael Anderson, "Our Youth Need You," Orthodox Church in America, https://oca.org/the-hub/study guides/our-youth-need-you1 (January 18, 2013).
[119] See Morgan and Stevens, *Simply Strategic Volunteers*, 113-115.
[120] Morgan and Stevens, *Simply Strategic Volunteers*, 34- 35; Hybels, *The Volunteer Revolution*, 39-43.

glory. Volunteering in a youth ministry program should never be about egos, but about the mission and vision of the Church—all for God's glory.[121]

Finding "committed" volunteers can sometimes be challenging, but each member of the Church desires to be a part of something that matters.[122] Thus, a spiritually mature Church member, will inevitably feel a need to be plugged into the Church ministry in some meaningful way. The commitment level of the volunteer will likely correlate with how much the servant is uniquely gifted in working with youth.[123] If it is not a good fit, both the youth ministry program and the individual volunteer suffer. In order to ensure a good level of commitment, parishes should make it easy for congregation members to informally and temporarily be involved in the youth ministry program to discover whether or not it is what

---

[121] Morgan and Stevens, *Simply Strategic Volunteers*, 67-68.
[122] Hybels, *The Volunteer Revolution*, 11-12.
[123] Hybels, *The Volunteer Revolution*, 18-19; Morgan and Stevens, *Simply Strategic Volunteers*, 59-60.

God designed them to do.[124] Whether it be a shadowing program, a "pre-servants" program, or some other temporary involvement, allowing Congregation members to try it out before committing will increase the likelihood of committed servants who take their role seriously.[125] It is not unreasonable to expect commitment from servants as long as there is opportunity to first make an informed decision to commit to the program.[126]

The commitment made, however, should be finite and never feel like a "life sentence."[127] Leaders should clearly lay out a timeline in which

---

[124] *See* Hybels, *The Volunteer Revolution*, 67-68, 81-82 (encouraging people to "experiment" with service to discover their spiritual talents); *see also* Morgan and Stevens, *Strategic Volunteers*, 41-42 (talking about letting people observe a ministry before committing to it).

[125] Youssef, interview (describing pre-servants classes).

[126] Fields, *Purpose Driven Youth Ministry*, 194-195 (explaining that a big part of Youth Ministry is building relationships with the kids, which cannot happen if the volunteers are not committed to showing up and bringing their passion with them); *see also* Morgan and Stevens, *Simply Strategic Volunteers*, 215-216.

[127] Morgan and Stevens, *Simply Strategic Volunteers*, 174-175.

the servant is committing to: one school year, one summer program, a retreat, or some other designated period of time. Too often strong members of the Church decline volunteering because the commitment level is not appropriately communicated or defined. Strategically, a one-school year commitment is appropriate to foster growing relationships between the students and the volunteers. A good Church leader, moreover, will always be on the lookout to develop and disciple volunteers into true spiritual leaders.[128]

In selecting volunteers, it is also important to keep in mind that these servants will be representing the Church and, therefore, need to have a Godly attitude. To that child, the volunteer may be the only face of the Church that they really interact with on a regular basis. If done right, this individual will move the child into many relationships within the Church community,

---

[128] Fields, *Purpose Driven Youth Ministry*, Ch. 15; see also Youssef, Interview.

including with the parish priest. Servants need to have the attitude that they strive to be a blessing to the Church, not a burden.[129] Indeed, volunteers should be expected to look for ways to be a blessing to others in their service.[130]

In short, in selecting volunteers, churches should not be timid with placing clear expectations on the servants and allow for volunteers to leave the ministry if they are not able to fulfill the expectations. The servants will be the face of the youth ministry, and any program implemented will only succeed insofar as the servants chosen are a good match, both spiritually and vocationally.

---

[129] See *e.g.*, Morgan and Stevens, *Simply Strategic Volunteers*, 209 (discussing how a continual bad attitude will bring the entire team down and may be a valid reason to "fire" a volunteer).

[130] Morgan and Stevens, *Simply Strategic Volunteers*, 19, 57 (discussing how sometimes volunteer duties will include "grunt work" or duties outside the specific "job description" such as picking up trash, putting chairs away, etc. Ideal volunteers are ones that bless the Church with a good attitude and seeking ways to be a blessing).

Equipping Volunteers

A great volunteer culture will not happen by accident; it always requires a major investment by Church staff.[131] It is a shame when committed, spiritually mature volunteers are selected for a youth ministry program that has no vision or resources to offer them.[132] Equipping the volunteers should begin before volunteers are actually selected. Leaders will have more success if they have a framework in place so the volunteers feel that their time is not wasted and that the leaders are consistently encouraging them in the service, but also investing in them outside the service.[133]

---

[131] Hybels, *The Volunteer Revolution*, 113; *see also* Messeh, interview (indicating that youth ministry is one of the most important facets of his church and, therefore, was worth investing resources in, to include a paid staff member).

[132] "Too many willing-hearted volunteers...show up to serve and discover they have nothing to do; an unprepared volunteer coordinator has wasted their time, causing them to lose precious hours they had willingly carved out from their busy schedule." Hybels, *The Volunteer Revolution*, 25; *see also* Morgan and Stevens, *Simply Strategic Volunteers*, 89-90 (talking about respecting volunteers' time).

[133] See Hybels, *The Volunteer Revolution*, 113- 118.

Practically speaking, volunteers want to be equipped and trained with resources that set them up for success.[134] With regard to Sunday school or other teaching, for example, equipping the volunteers with meaningful training and detailed lesson plans is imperative to set the volunteer up for success. It minimizes the amount of prep work volunteers have to do and it maintains the quality of the youth program.

As discussed in Part II, *infra*, many Coptic Orthodox parishes in North America do not currently operate this way. Rather, lesson planning is generally an expected duty of a Coptic volunteer.[135] The perspective from many Coptic parishes is that volunteers must take their role seriously, invest the time and prayer to properly prepare for their lesson, and allow for the Holy Spirit to work.[136]

The perspective is certainly valid as the

---

[134] Morgan and Stevens, *Simply Strategic Volunteers*, 21.
[135] Youssef, interview; Messeh, interview; Hanna, interview.
[136] Ibid.

spiritual life of the volunteer is crucial. Removing the task of lesson planning from volunteers, however, *can* be done without taking away the importance of the volunteer's role and will clearly provide substantial benefit to youth ministry. Lesson-plans made by a group of individuals skilled in education, child psychology, human development, and theology, clearly offers the benefit of well-thought out lessons that are theologically sound and age-appropriate, ensuring a continuity in learning and quality. The benefits of this approach are clear.

Volunteers equipped with lesson plans, moreover, must still take their role seriously as any lesson plan will still require proper reading and preparation. A volunteer should also be trained on *how* to effectively use a lesson plan. Overall, the lesson plan should be thought of as a tool to a volunteer and not a substitute from his or her own preparations.

In addition, it is important to keep in mind the ultimate role of the volunteer. Leaders are selecting volunteer servants not for their ability to write lesson plans, but rather for their spiritual maturity and gifts of working with the youth. The prong being emphasized through the servants is "the Reality of God" prong. It is not through the servants' efforts that we hope for the youth to gain spiritual *knowledge*, but rather to gain spiritual *role models* and have opportunities to experience the reality of God. Spiritual knowledge is accomplished from properly selecting youth ministry materials as well as partnering with families and equipping families to continue this education at home.[137]

Equipping volunteers must also include a great deal of pastoral care encouraging, training, edifying, and routinely building up the servants.[138] Volunteers should be required to

---

[137] See also Part III, "CONNECT WITH FAMILIES," *supra.*
[138] Joseph J. Allen, *The Ministry of the Church: The Image of Pastoral Care* (Yonkers: St. Vladimir's Seminary Press, 1986), 22-25, 97-98 (comparing the priest to a shepherd. As Jesus was our shepherd, so too are priests called to have a direct and personal relationship with the flock of his church).

have a spiritual father for confession in which they are regularly meeting with and participating in the Sacrament of Confession.[139] Leaders and priests should make some effort to be cognizant of volunteers' lives outside of youth ministry and find ways to show that they care. Sometimes there is a temptation to treat the Church service like a job, but volunteers should never feel like mere workforce. Relationships matter and giving of time to engage, inspire, motivate, and encourage parish volunteers is vital for both the ministry and the individual volunteer.[140] Leaders should also continually think of ways to show volunteer appreciation—either through events or simple gestures.[141] Equipping volunteers includes finding ways to remind them that what they are

---

[139] Hybels, *The Volunteer Revolution*, 129-130 (talking about how servant hood longevity requires healthy self-care); Allen, *The Ministry of the Church*, Ch. 4.
[140] Morgan and Stevens, *Strategic Volunteers*, 32-33; Hybels, *The Volunteer Revolution*, 113-114.
[141] *See* Hybels, *The Volunteer Revolution* at 126-127; Hybels, *Strategic Volunteers* at 27 (talking about the importance of regularly praising and encouraging volunteers that are doing a good job).

doing is valuable and appreciated.[142]

In short, successful selection and equipping of volunteers should be cognizant of the purpose of the volunteer, which is primarily to assist the youth experience the "Reality of God" by selecting authentic and good spiritual role models. God gave spiritual gifts to "...some to be apostles, some prophets, some evangelists, and some pastors and teachers...."[143] The Church should do its part by not only identifying ideal volunteers, but nourishing those relationships and equipping them for success.

Body of Christ: Helping Youth Discover Their Unique Place

Koulomzin's "Body of Christ" prong is aimed at helping youth discover his or her belonging in the Body of Christ.[144] In other words, youth ministry should include meaningful

---

[142] Hybels, *The Volunteer Revolution* at 117-118.
[143] Ephesians 4:11 (NKJV).
[144] Koulomzin, *Our Church and Our Children*, 23-24.

programs that help youth discover their unique passions, talents, and identity in the Orthodox Faith.

Youth ministry in any particular Coptic Orthodox parish in North America today might contain youth groups, sports groups, deacon classes, or other programs, but undoubtedly the main focus of youth ministry will consistently be Sunday school.

In contrast, a well-rounded youth ministry program ought to think beyond Sunday school and implement non Sunday programs that will assist the youth discover their unique talents and passions. Programs offering opportunities to serve the community or volunteer within a church ministry, for example, are ways a parish can help its youth discover their God-given passions and talents. Parishes should also not discount the importance of fellowship opportunities. Youth need "childish amusement" a place to let off steam and freedom from responsibilities.¹⁴⁵ If the Church provides a place for the youth to fill this need, then it can help youth resist the temptation filling this need in more destructive places. The Orthodox Church is one unified Body of Christ, and this ought to include children. Youth need to be given opportunities to feel a sense of belonging and ownership in the Church.¹⁴⁶

This unity of congregation is particularly important in the Orthodox Church where many youth are first generation American struggling to fit in at school and in their world in general.¹⁴⁷ The wholeness of the Church, clergy

---

¹⁴⁵ Sr. Magdalen, *Children in the Church Today*, 71-74.

¹⁴⁶ Michael Anderson, "Is Your Area Meeting the Needs of Your Youth?," Orthodox Church in America, https://oca.org/the-hub/about-youth-ministry/is-your-area-meeting-the-needs-of-your-youth (accessed September 11, 2018); John L. Boojamra, *Foundations for Christian Education* (New York: St. Vladimir's Seminary Press, 1989), 29-30 (explaining that the entire Church is the educator; youth cannot learn about "how" to be a Christian, but rather have opportunities to live out their faith).

¹⁴⁷ Anderson, "Is Your Area Meeting the Needs of Your Youth?" (discussing American Orthodox kids feeling as though they are "the only one of their kind.").

participation, and teaching the kids that they are part of one Body in Christ is a key component of the Orthodox youth ministry vision.[148]

A parish ought to spend time ensuring any and all programs and/or curriculum chosen are appropriate to facilitate spiritual growth as well as opportunities for the youth to find their place in the Body of Christ. Programs, moreover, should be focused on teaching youth how to apply theological principles to their everyday life versus mere memorization.[149] The bottom line of every youth ministry program implemented should be, "what message will they apply when they go home?"[150]

---

[148] See Koulomzin, "Children and Christian Education" (where she discusses the importance of teaching children to take their knowledge about God and their gifts and talents given by God, and offer it back to the world).

[149] Boojamra, *Foundations for Christian Education*, 42-44 (discussing the importance of combining Christian education with experiences for the child to apply the education to his/her reality).

[150] Koulomzin, *Our Church and Our Children*, 47; *see also* Gaskins, *I Believe In...*, 21 (A Catholic teenager shares his experience being involved in Catholic Youth Organization (CYO)).

Identity formation is part of adolescence, and as our youth grow and discover their unique gifts, talents, and personalities, the Church should provide avenues in which they can experience their potential within the Body of Christ.[151] Creating meaningful programs will require the parish to be aware of student culture, and give students opportunities to participate in community service, evangelism, fellowship, worship, peer mentorship, and so forth to discover their unique and essential connection to the Body of Christ.[152]

The content of the program, moreover, will never be as important as the substance of the people running the programs. Spiritually led role-models are instrumental in helping the youth learn how to fully participate in the liturgical and community life of the parish. For example, in

---

[151] Boojamra, *Foundations for Christian Education*, 47-48; Fields, *Purpose Driven Youth Ministry*, 87-93 (discussing the different kinds of personalities that tend to make up the youth – those drawn to community service, evangelism, fellowship, worship, etc.).

[152] See Fields, *Purpose Driven Youth Ministry*, Ch. 6-10.

Gaskins' book, *I Believe In...*, a young Catholic man shared his experience being involved in the Catholic Youth Organization (CYO) as follows,

> "CYO was the only thing that kept me in Catholicism. I saw fellowship happening, I saw people doing things for people—I thought, this is what Christianity is about. I didn't get that out of mass or just reading the Bible."[153]

What is compelling about this experience is that this young man experienced Christian faith not through a class, but through a fellowship program designed to have youth live out their faith in practical experiences. So too Coptic parishes in North America should be encouraged to create meaningful programs designed to have youth live out their faith in service, evangelism, fellowship, and mentorship.[154]

---

[153] Gaskins, *I Believe In...*, 21.
[154] Anderson, "Is Your Area Meeting the Needs of Your Youth?" (discussing and encouraging Orthodox Youth Ministry to create local activities as well as Regional activities with other parishes, such as camps or conferences); Anderson, "Our Youth Need You" (emphasizing that programs should be meaningful and not

Christ must be in the center of it all: genuine life, true and real life in perfection and abundance, is found only in the Church of Christ.[155] Thus, while creating well rounded programs is the goal, the youth ministry effort must strike a careful balance between implementing fun, humor, modern culture, and activities with the authenticity of the Orthodox Church.[156] Koulomzin makes a beautiful comparison between youth ministry and the Holy Eucharist:

> "In the Holy Eucharist God accepts our gifts and gives us Himself in Holy Communion. We offer ourselves to Him. He gives Himself to us. And at the very end we leave the church. We do not stay on and

---

merely made for the sake of programs); see also Boojamra, *Foundations for Christian Education*, 7-10 (explaining that the entire Church is the educator and that children should be exposed to the Church life).

[155] Orthodox Church of America, "The Church," The Orthodox Faith, Vol. IV, Spirituality, Orthodox Spirituality, https://oca.org/orthodoxy/the-orthodox faith/spirituality/orthodox-spirituality/the-church (accessed Sept. 11, 2018).

[156] See *e.g.*, Fields, *Purpose Driven Youth Ministry*, 125- 126; 137-140; 156-160.

> on. We go back to the world, to the life that is not enclosed in the church building. We try to live out in our life that which we have received."[157]

It is imperative that a portion of youth ministry be dedicated to encouraging youth to give back to others. Perhaps some youth will be naturally talented at peer mentorship, but other youth will find their passion in community service or other types of projects.[158] Aiding the youth to find their place in the Body of Christ adds another important dimension to any youth ministry effort in a parish—it teaches the youth to fulfill God's commandment to be a light in the World and preach His holy name to all nations.

Religious Education: Partnering with Parents

[Y]outh ministry that excludes parents is about as effective as a Band-Aid on a

---

[157] Koulomzin, "Children and Christian Education."
[158] See *e.g.*, Strommen, *Five Cries of Youth*, 52-71 (discussing the "Cry of Social Protest" describing youth naturally passionate about social injustice).

hemorrhage.¹⁵⁹ Koulomzin's "religious education" prong pertains to the technical understanding provided to the youth of the Orthodox faith.¹⁶⁰ The importance of family involvement in this prong, however, cannot be understated but too often, a youth ministry effort in a parish completely separates parents from the equation.

Religious education tends to be thought of as synonymous with Sunday school. In that limited viewpoint, however, the most youth ministry can hope to engage a child is one hour per week (if even that much). The remainder of the time, that child is with his or her family. The parent-child relationship must not be undermined. Studies seem to consistently show that the parent-child relationship is one of the most important factors with regard to moral and ethical issues.¹⁶¹ The youth ought to be receiving

---

[159] Fields, *Purpose Driven Youth Ministry*, 251.
[160] Koulomzin, *Our Church and Our Children*, 24-26.
[161] See Purpura, *Moral and Ethical Issues*, 48-50; Harakas, *Contemporary Moral Issues*, 103; Boojamra, *Foundations of*

the majority of their spiritual education from their parents. Thus it is imperative that youth ministry utilizes that partnership so that whatever is being taught at church is reinforced at home and vice-versa. The Church also has a crucial opportunity to encourage parents not to underestimate their significance and to equip them with the resources needed to continue their child's spiritual education at home.[162]

Youth ministry efforts in the Church should include a family ministry component, providing guidance, support, and resources to parents.[163] It is of upmost importance that family life stay consistent with the values taught on Sundays and that the family emulates the love of

---

Christian Education, 63-64 (discussing the Church's failure to properly consider the family as primary educators of the youth).

[162] Harakas, *Contemporary Moral Issues*, 75; Harakas, *Living the Faith*, 246-249; Boojamra, *Foundations for Christian Education*, 64 (discussing parents as the primary educator for their children).

[163] See also Koulomzin, *Our Church and Our Children*, Ch. 3 (discussing the importance of family ministry to provide guidance and support to parents).

Christ. Additionally, many youth struggle with family issues, and the Church should be a safe place to turn for help and guidance.[164] Children with a historically positive parish life experience with a Christian family, are more likely to stay in their Orthodox faith into adulthood.[165]

Volunteers, in turn, should be expected to foster an open-communication culture with the parents. While some volunteers may be "timid" or otherwise "intimidated" by parents (especially of teens), Orthodox churches should foster a oneness in community, encouraging parent involvement and providing family resources and/or events for the whole church to be involved. The fact of the matter is, parents with similarly aged children are going to share similar fears, concerns, and overall values and it does little to keep them out of the youth ministry equation.[166] More often than not, parents want to

---

[164] Strommen, *Five Cries of Youth*, 33-51.
[165] Sr. Magdalen, *Children in the Church Today*, 01-02.
[166] Fields, *Purpose Driven Youth Ministry*, Ch. 14.

be involved in the spiritual education of their child, but a lot of times are not sure how.[167] While it is nice for youth to have their own activities at the parish some of the time, it is necessary to also have avenues for the families to come together in the parish and lean on each other as well as the youth ministry leaders for support.

Practically speaking, youth ministry efforts should think through how they will communicate with parents on what their child learned and how to continue the learning at home—whether it be weekly handouts or a parent-resource website or some other consistent mechanism.[168] Youth ministry should perhaps partner with a family ministry effort at the parish to identify important social topics and provide resources and/or lectures on those topics

---

[167] Fields, *Purpose Driven Youth Ministry*, 261-268; see also Boojamra, *Foundations of Christian Education*, 68 (quoting St. Basil on the importance of the Church community helping each other, supporting each other's needs, and working together as one Body in Christ).

[168] See *e.g.*, St. Timothy & St. Athanasius Coptic Orthodox Church, "Parent Resource Page," http://stsa.church/parents (accessed August 17, 2018).

for parents.[169] Youth ministry, with the leadership of the parish priest, should also encompass a pastoral care component for families that are deeply struggling and need extra support. It is imperative that parents are knowledgeable of what the Church teaches about major social and ethical issues, and also well equipped with resources. Overall, there should be a teamwork mentality with parents and youth ministry and an open-communication culture.[170]

Staying Current: Ongoing Efforts to Understand Current Youth Needs

"I cannot learn anything that does not interest me."[171] Clearly a youth ministry effort will not be successful in any vision if it does not stay up to date on current youth needs.

---

[169] See *e.g.,* St. Mary & St. Athanasius Coptic Orthodox Church, "The PEP Talks," http://www.ThePEPTALKS.org (accessed Sept. 11, 2018).
[170] Fields, *Purpose Driven Youth Ministry,* 251-268.
[171] Erikson, *Identity Youth and Crisis,* 144.

In addition to the five-prongs discussed herein, parishes ought to invoke some ongoing strategy to regularly review, update, and enhance programs and materials used. Youth culture is continually evolving and while the Orthodox faith is indeed ancient and unchanging, the application in our lives continually evolves. For example, Biblical and Orthodox principles of controlling your tongue remain unchanged, but in today's world the application of this principle ought to include a discussion of social media, texting, and cyber-bullying.[172] Similarly, the Biblical and Orthodox principles of sexual purity remains unchanged, but in the growing age of Internet access and laws around gender and sexual orientation, the topic would be incomplete without also discussing the dangers of Internet pornography, homosexuality, "sexting," and gender

---

[172] Purpura, *Moral and Ethical Issues*, 16-20.

identity.[173] Thus, one cannot merely have a set-in-stone program that is not continually being reviewed and updated to stay current with the changing times.

Leaders and volunteers, additionally, ought to strike a balance between being genuine to who they are, but at the same time staying acquainted with youth culture. As St. Paul said in 1 Corinthians 9:22, "I have become all things to all men, that I might by all means save some."[174] So to the youth, the leaders and volunteers should invest some time becoming knowledgeable with and interested in youth needs in order to better help them. Being in tune with current culture empowers volunteers to be better mentors.[175] Koloumzin, in *Our Church and Our Children*, discusses how our entire

---

[173] Ibid., 73-76.
[174] 1 Corinthians 9:22 (NKJV).
[175] Michael Anderson, "The Youth Friendly Parish," Orthodox Church in America, https://oca.org/parish ministry/yya/the-youth-friendly-parish (accessed Sept. 11, 2018).

culture has become divorced from religion and therefore the Orthodox youth ministry should be there to help bring them into the Church.[176] Many times, American-born Orthodox youth feel strange as if they are the "only one of their kind" at their school or secular atmospheres. The ministry should give them an opportunity to develop friendships with like-minded people.[177] On the other hand, Strommen, in the Five Cries of Youth, talks about how effective youth leaders should stay genuine and not try to pretend they are kids (or otherwise become big kids). Rather, they should act like adults, use their own experiences and vocabulary, and respect the autonomy of youth.[178] Essentially, youth crave steady and genuine adult role models. Adults attempting to be

---

[176] Kolomzin, *Our Church and Our Children*, 7.
[177] Anderson, "The Youth Friendly Parish."
[178] Strommen, *Five Cries of Youth*, 118-121; *see also* Erikson, *Identity Youth and Crisis*, 129 (where the author describes identity confusion amongst adolescence where, on the one hand, they express need for faith and trusting relationships, but on the other hand, express cynical mistrust).

kids will typically spawn mistrust amongst the youth, not to mention being awkward, out of place, and inappropriate. Parishes, then, ought to make an effort to address their youth's current struggles in program content, encourage adult and peer mentorship, and cultivate opportunities for like-minded Orthodox Christian youth to form bonds with each other. It is equally important for youth to have adult and youth role models/friendships they can rely on and utilize for edification in the current culture. The Church body ought to want to see the youth involved in Church and, in turn, youth naturally want to have purpose and be wanted.[179]

---

[179] Anderson, "The Youth Friendly Parish" (talking about not just ministering to the youth, but giving them real responsibilities to minister to others); *see also* Strommen, *Five Cries of Youth* (the book describes various "cries of youth," one of which is penned "the Cry of Joy," describing youth with a natural religious fervor – those with an overflow of a sense of identity and mission in love. These youth, Strommen proposes, are prime candidates to be peer mentors because it comes natural to them and they will facilitate a loving Church environment).

The youth are a vital part of our Church. It is important to properly invest in them and serve them. The youth that are part of the North American Coptic Orthodox parishes, moreover, have unique ethical and moral issues facing them. It is important that the Church learns how to effectively help its youth maneuver these issues, create a personal faith and relationship with Christ, and stay connected to the Body of Christ. Youth ministry should be a safe haven for youth to find like-minded peers, strong role models, and strong faith-based support to discover who they are and who they were meant to be in the Body of Christ.

Conclusion

There is a growing hunger in the Coptic Orthodox Church in North America—a hunger stemming from each younger, American-born generation. They seek belonging, identity, and direction. The Church has a short chance to help them form that identity in the Body of Christ through a well thought-out youth ministry effort, partnered with parents, before the youth find their identity and sense of belonging elsewhere.

Caring for the youth of the Church is neither solely the parents' responsibility nor is it a set of volunteer's sole responsibility either. Rather, if every person is truly a part of the Body of Christ, then that includes children too. Children should never feel that they are less important or a nuisance. They should be embraced as full members of the Body of Christ and drawn into participation as the integral parts they are.

The proposed new framework model for youth ministry outlined herein allows for flexibility for each parish to customize a program to fit the geographic and cultural needs of their flock, and also allows for enough uniformity that the Coptic Orthodox Church remains One Body in Christ.[180] It is further proposed that a Department of Education be formed and tasked with creating and continually updating consistent, theologically sound, and age-appropriate resources and curriculum universally available to all Coptic Orthodox parishes in North America. Such an effort

---

[180] See Appendix V for a table summary of the five prongs and recommendations made in this study.

would have significant benefit to our youth, providing quality and age-appropriate resources, and also properly equip volunteers to reach youth in an effective way.

The Coptic Orthodox Church started as an "immigrant church," but if it does not evolve, Orthodoxy will be eroded by each generation and it will become a cultural club.[181] Youth ministry in North American Coptic parishes requires a mind shift and a clear mission statement. The goal of any youth ministry effort should be to mentor and disciple our youth to form their own identity in the Church and their own personal faith with our Heavenly Father, Jesus Christ, and the Holy Spirit. It is the people—the clergy, the leaders, the volunteers, and the parents—that will make or break any youth ministry effort because it is their actions and the way they live out

---

[181] Koulomzin, *Our Church and Our Children*, stats p.11; see also Sorial, *Incarnational Exodus*, 12-13.

their faith that will matter most to the youth. As Koulomzin so eloquently states in her work, regardless of how strong a Sunday School curriculum may be, textbooks will not teach the youth how to become a "good" Orthodox Christian; "one must lead by example."[182]

---

[182] Koulomzin, *Our Church and Our Children*, 13.

Appendices

Appendix I

Elementary-Aged Catered Lesson Plan on Joseph[183]

Activate Goodness and Faithfulness

Bible story: Joseph Trusts God No Matter What (Full story Genesis 37-48)
SuperHolies Focus: Activate SuperHolies Goodness and Faithfulness to help you say no to bad choices and trust God no matter what.
Memory Verses: "But the fruit of the Spirit is love, joy, peace, longsuffering, kindness, goodness, faithfulness, gentleness, self-control. Against such there is no such law." Galatians 5:22-23, NKJV

1. **In God We Trust**

   What you need:
   - Pennies (enough for each child to have one)
   - Joseph Synopsis (in lesson plan)
   - Bible or Age-Appropriate

---

[183] This lesson plan, penned by the author, comes from excerpts of "Philo & the SuperHolies VBS," available at https://bridgestoorthodoxy.com/collections/pathways/products/philo-the-superholies-vbs-1 (accessed Sept. 28, 2020).

Storybook to read "Joseph and Potiphar's Wife" story or show the video (video link can be found in "Extras" document)

What you do:
- Sit in a circle and pass out the pennies. Ask them to look at the pennies closely and tell you what it says.
- "In God We Trust!" Ask: What do you think that means? *Solicit answers then explain that today's story is all about trusting God even when we do not know what will happen, even when bad things could happen, even when we have a lot to worry about.*
- Say: "When I pause the story and put my penny up in the air, I want you all to shout: 'In God We Trust!' Can we try that?" *Practice putting your penny up in the air and having them shout "In God We Trust!"*

Joseph had eleven brothers; he was the second youngest and only a teenager at the start of our story. Although parents should not have favorites, Joseph was his father's favorite son. In fact, Jacob gave his son Joseph a coat with many colors on it. When Joseph's brothers saw the coat, they were very jealous and would not even speak to him. But...

Pause and put your penny up and have the kids say, "In God We Trust!"

That is right—Joseph trusted God even when his brothers were mean to him. God talked to Joseph in an unusual way—through his dreams. Joseph dreamt of sheaves of wheat in the field bowed down to his sheave and another dream where stars in the sky bowed down to his star. He...

Pause and put your penny up and have the kids say, "In God We Trust!"

Yes! He trusted in God. So much so, that he shared the dreams with his brothers. Well, his brothers got even more jealous of him and hated him even more. Out of jealousy—they did something terrible. They threw him in the pit—they wanted to kill him, but one of his brothers (Ruben) talked them out of it. He was planning on rescuing Joseph later, but before he had a chance, his brothers sold Joseph to men traveling to Egypt.

Pause and put your penny up and have the kids say, "In God We Trust!"

Joseph seemed to be in a pretty bad situation—but as we see in the next part of the story, he never stopped trusting in God and did not worry about his situation.

His brothers even tricked his dad—they grabbed Joseph's coat of many colors and rubbed animal blood in it to make it look like a wild animal had killed Joseph. When Jacob saw the coat, he cried for many days and no one could make him feel better.

Now pay attention closely to what happens to Joseph in Egypt because I think it may help our friend Philo:
- Play video

What you say (after the video):
- Joseph faced a lot of troubles and most of the time it was not his fault. He trusted God no matter what and always said no to bad choices, even if it meant he would go to jail! Chances are if Joseph did whatever Potiphar's wife wanted him to do, he may have avoided prison—but Joseph cared more about pleasing God than about avoiding jail. In the end, trusting God was exactly what he needed to do. God had a plan to make sure no one would be hungry, to make sure Joseph would reconcile with his family, and to make sure the Israelites would be safe from the Egyptians.
- No matter what—when we stay faithful to God and trust in His goodness, then whether times are easy or times are hard—we can be sure that in the end God has plan and it will be our good!

- Review Philo's Super Challenge and discuss how Joseph's story could help Philo with his problem
- By choosing his relationship with God over anything else, Philo is doing the right thing. Sometimes doing the right thing is not the easy choice. What we saw with Joseph is that for a while it seemed like he was almost getting "punished" for doing the right thing. We should never let ourselves be tricked into thinking that. God loves us more than anyone else and His plan is much better than the plans we have for ourselves. Even if Philo has to miss out on something fun, his relationship with God is much more valuable than basketball! I know it is not easy to choose to trust God, especially when you are not sure how it will turn out. The SuperHolies are there to give us courage to say no to bad choices and trust God no matter what!

2. **Draw a Twin**

   What you need:
   - Construction paper (one per child)
   - Pencils (one per child)

   What you do: Tell the kids you will be passing out paper and pencils and splitting them up into pairs.

One child will draw a picture (but not show it to their partner). Instead, they need to describe to their partner what they need to draw to try to make it look as much alike as their drawing.

For example, call one chile up to the front of the class. (*Draw a sun on your construction paper—show the class but do not show the child volunteer*). Give the child volunteer a construction paper and a marker. Give instruction on how to draw a twin drawing. (*Examples: Draw a big circle. Now, draw a small triangle at the top/outside of the circle. Draw another upside down triangle on the bottom outside of the circle. Draw another triangle on the left side of the circle, and on the right side. Draw a diagonal line between each triangle, etc.*).

When you are done, show the class both drawings and ask them whether they are "twins."

Now, break up the class into pairs so they can try the same activity. They can flip their papers over and switch roles if there is time.

Once you give them time to do their drawings, come back together in a circle for people to share "twin" drawings.

What you say: What was easy and what was hard about this activity? *Let kids share.*

Our relationship with God is very similar to the exercise we did. God knows the big picture and He has a plan for us. He tell us pieces as we go along, and we have to trust Him and rely on His Holy Word so that in the end, His will is complete in us. When I told my volunteer to draw a big circle—he probably did not know what he was drawing yet. If he decided to draw a rectangle instead of a circle, well, that would have been a weird looking sun.

Sometimes when we get scared or worry about something, we are tempted to stay away from God's direction. I want you to remember this exercise and Joseph's story. God saw the big picture: He saw Joseph being in charge of the food, He saw Pharaoh giving Joseph an important job, He saw past Joseph's troubles with his brothers, Potiphar, and the jail cell.

Just like our friends who were giving directions to our drawers—God sees a perspective we do not have. Trusting God, no matter what, means we never have to worry because God will take care of you. When we feel worried or anxious about something, remember to do the sign of the cross, activate the SuperHolies Goodness and Faithfulness and remember to say no to bad choices and trust God no matter what!

3. **Memory Verse Hula-Hoop Pass**

   What you need:
   - One Hula-Hooper about 10-12 kids. If you have a large class, you may consider 2 hula-hoops with 2 groups doing the activity at the same time
   - Bible

   What you do:
   - **First:** practice looking up Galatians 5:22-23 in a Bible
     - It is really important that kids know how to find a verse in the Bible
     - Tips: have one student come up to the front and hand him/her the Bible
     - Explain that when you open the Bible to the middle, the Old Testament will be to the left, and the New Testament to the right
     - Galatians is in the New Testament, so we know we have to move to the right
     - The beginning of the New

Testament are the Gospels: Matthew, Mark, Luke, and John (the Gospels tell us the story of Christ)
- o After the Gospels comes the Acts of the Apostles, and then the epistles of St. Paul
- o Galatians is one of St. Paul's epistles
- o Once they find the proper book in the Bible, explain that the "5" is the chapter (the Big Number) and "22-23" are the verses (the Little Numbers)
- o Give the student a high-five when they find the verse
- o Give at least 2 students a chance to find the verse (you can choose 2 different students for each session during the week!)

- **Second:** Play Memory Verse Hula-Hoop Pass
    - o Have the kids stand in a circle holding hands with the hula-hoop starting interlaced on one end
    - o The idea is they have to wiggle their way through the hula-hoop and pass it all around the circle without

letting go of their hands
- Start off saying, "But the fruit of the Spirit is..." then wiggle the hula-hoop to the next child
- When the hula-hoop reaches a child, they should say all the fruits of the Spirit, and then wiggle around the hula-hoop and pass it to the next person. By the end of the circle, everyone should have had a turn in saying the memory verse (*If you have a big class, you might want to have 2 circles going with 2 separate hula-hoop passes for the sake of time*).
- Keep playing rounds. For the first round, have the kids practice the Memory Verse. For the second round, have the kids try to remember what "Peace" gives them power to do. (Conquer fears)—so each kid should say "Peace helps me conquer my fears" when the hula-hoop is passed to them, and then they wiggle to pass it to the next person. For the third round, focus on "Kindness and Goodness"

gives us the power "to be kind and tender to everyone." For the fourth round, focus on "Love and Joy" gives us the power to "love and be happy no matter what." For the fifth round, focus on "Patience and Self-Control" gives us the power to "wait even if we do not want to." For the sixth round, focus on "Goodness and Faithfulness" gives us the power to "say no to bad choices and trust God no matter what."

Note: you can do the first three rounds for session 1, and the second three rounds during session 2.

What you say: Can you believe we are the end of the week? I hope you guys keep these SuperHolies in mind whenever you need some extra Super Strength with your own Super Challenge in life. Just like our friend Philo, the SuperHolies are there to help you too! Let's make the sign of the cross and activate them now as we close in prayer.

Close in prayer and then dismiss them to the next activity.

Appendix II

Teen Catered Lesson Plan on Joseph[184]

In God We Trust: Abide

Bible story: Interpreting Dreams (*Genesis 40-41*)
The Takeaway: Abide in God's Love because, to Him, we are Never Forgotten
Key Verse: "Those who trust in the Lord are like Mount Zion, which cannot be shaken but endures forever."

1. Opener IceBreaker (Inventions and Inventors)
   - Trivia Slides (contains inventions we use ALL time, but we probably have forgotten the name of the invention and/or the inventor). You can divide the class up into teams, but this is one that is fun to do as a whole class.

Leader: "Welcome back everyone! This month we have been following the unfortunate events in the life of Joseph. But, no matter what happened to him, he trusted in God. Our series about trusting God is called "In God We Trust."

---

[184] This example lesson-plan is an excerpt from a month-long teen unit called "In God We Trust" written by the author and available at http://bridgestoorthodoxy.com/collections/crossroads (last accessed September 28, 2020).

CG Slide: Theme Slide

This series is really a "how-to" series. We know we should trust God, but sometimes it can be hard to do. Maybe God is taking too long to answer a prayer. Maybe things are happening that seem hopeless. Maybe you do not like losing control. This series is designed to help us get better at trusting God. Let us review what we have learned so far:

CG Slide: Past Week's Takeaways

Week 1, if you remember, everyone let Joseph down. His dad played favorites, which created a bad situation with his brothers; his brothers' grudges, which led to really terrible actions; and even Joseph let himself down by boasting about his dream. So the first step in trusting God was to realize that people let you down and instead put our HOPE in God's goodness, which will never fail you.

Week 2, Joseph fled from temptation and obeyed God's commandments no matter what situation he found himself in—even when it was not an easy choice. And because he kept God first, God blessed Joseph. The loyalty of people is fleeting, but God stays loyal no matter what. Step 2 to trusting God is OBEYING His commandments no matter what because once again, God will stay loyal to us even when others do not.

Today we are going to look at the next stop on HOW to trust God through Joseph's story: Joseph abided in God's unwavering LOVE because no matter what, God did not forget Joseph.

Speaking of FORGETTING, that reminds me of our game for today!

CG Slides: Inventions and Inventors

Leader: In a minute, I am going to show you some trivia slides of inventions we use ALL the time, but perhaps we have forgetting either what the invention is called or what the invention is used for. Let's see how much you know!

CG: Trivia Slides

After the game:
Leader: It is interesting, is it not? Something we use regularly, like windshield wipers, but we never give two seconds thought as to who invented it or the history behind it.

Everyone will have moments in their life when they will feel underappreciated, undervalued, or just plain forgotten. It is important that we fight these thoughts because they are a sort of illusion. None of us have any bad feelings towards these inventors and by using these inventions we do have an appreciation for their creation even if we do not remember who invented them.

The point of doing good things is not to be remembered, but because it is pleasing to God. And God never forgets us. To us, it is not the *things* we do or invent that matter as much as the *heart* of the person. To God, we are invaluable and precious.

2. Video/Trust Lesson (Joseph is forgotten but not by God)

Leader: Last week, Potiphar threw Joseph in jail because Potiphar's wife accused him of something he did not do. What is interesting though, is that Potiphar threw Joseph in the royal prison and allowed him to hold a position of authority there. All of this suggests that Potiphar (Pharaoh's Captain of the Guard) most likely had his doubts about Joseph's guilt.

In any case, God did not leave Joseph. Today we are going to talk about several dreams Joseph interpreted. Through God, Joseph had the ability to interpret dreams, and through this ability others would see God's glory. But would they remember Joseph? Let's take a look at the first couple of dreams Joseph interpreted.

Play video.

After video:
Leader: Let's review a couple of key points. First, Joseph was in prison for a few years before he got the company of the cupbearer/butler and the

baker. After Joseph interprets their dreams, he asks something of the cupbearer.

CG Slide: Genesis 40:14-15

Leader: Joseph says, "God gave me the ability to interpret your dream and it is good news. All I ask of you is to remember me." The story then goes on to say that what Joseph interpreted came true. The cupbearer was restored to his position, and the baker was hanged. Did the cupbearer remember Joseph?

CG Slide: Genesis 40:23

Leader: No, Joseph was forgotten. From Genesis 41, which you will read in Small Groups today, we know that two years passed before the cupbearer remembered Joseph. Here's what I want you to remember: when we trust God, that means we trust and abide in His love for us. His love for us is not like human love though. He does not love us because of who we are, but rather, He loves us because of who He is.

It is a lot like our invention game. We do not care about the details of where Velcro came from, but God care immensely about that person because of who God is. And who is God? God is love.

That is another piece of the puzzle of "HOW." How can we trust God? We can trust God by ABIDING in HIS LOVE that He will never forget us. And that is our Takeaway for today.

CG Slide: The Takeaway: ABIDE in His Love because to Him, we are NEVER forgotten.

In Genesis 41, something happens that could only be the hand of God that jolted the cupbearer's memory—does anyone know what happened?

Give the students a chance to respond.

Leader: Pharaoh had two dreams that were puzzling, concerning, and one that no one could interpret. All of a sudden, the cupbearer had the memory jog he needed. From where we stand, it is easy to see God's hand in this situation, right?

What I hope we learn from Joseph, who sat in prison for several years, is that we can always abide in God's Love. In the most hopeless, bad, lost, and evil circumstances, God is still working and He loves us and will not forget or abandon us.

CG Slide: Key Verse

> **Key Verse:** "Those who trust in the Lord are like Mount Zion, which cannot be shaken but endures forever." Psalm 125:1

Joseph's story really shows you how invincible he was because of his trust in God.

3. Discussion Questions
    - Have you ever felt undervalued, underappreciated, or just plain forgotten?
    - While none of us has probably never been in jail, have you ever waited a really long time for an answer to a prayer? Have you ever felt like God forgot you? Explain your answer.
    - Why do you think the cupbearer forgot Joseph? (*No right or wrong answer here—just brainstorming why we often forget about those who have helped us*).
    - In the Inventions activity we saw that we often do not "see" people beyond what they've done for us. How is God's love different? (*The point here is for teens to see that human affection is often self-serving but God's love is selfless*).
    - In Large Group, the leader said: "God does not love you because of who you are; He loves us because of Who He is." What does that mean to you?
    - Open your Bible and read Psalm 125:1. In what ways do you feel abiding in God's love for you make you invincible? (*Emphasize God's love is unconditional, unchanging,*

and undeserved).

Let us close in prayer.

4. Pray and dismiss

Appendix III

Elementary-Aged Catered Lesson Plan on the Sacrament of Communion[185]

Communion

Bible Story: Various passages (main ones: John 6:53-64; Matthew 26:26-28)
Key Verse: "He who eats My Flesh and drinks My Blood abides in Me, and I in him." (John 6:56)
Bottom Line: Communion is the sacrament that crowns all the other sacraments. It is our way of abiding in the Body of Christ.

1. **Opener/Ice Breaker: Eat, Drink, and Be Merry**

    What you need:
    - Ritz crackers
    - Pad of paper
    - Pen for each team

For this game, you will need to split the class in two teams. Each team needs Ritz crackers, a pad of paper, and a pen. **Please use caution and your best judgment while playing to keep the kids**

---

[185] This lesson-plan was written by the author from the "tween" unit called "The Sacrament Olympics." For the full curriculum unit, see https://bridgestoorthodoxy.com/collections/arches (last accessed September 28, 2020).

safe.

Each team will have a designated "clue giver." The clue giver has to fill their mouth with Ritz crackers while trying to say the Key Verse out loud. The first team to write down the Key Verse correctly wins. Be sure to give the Clue Giver the Key Verse written out on a piece of paper. (See above: John 6:56, "He who eats My Flesh and drinks My Blood abides in Me, and I in him.")

Leader: Good morning and welcome! Today, we are continuing our unit on the Seven Sacraments. Last week, we talked about Baptism and Chrismation. To introduce our Sacrament topic today, let us start with a little game called Eat, Drink, and Be Merry. First, let us split up into teams.

Play the game as described above and then give the Clue Givers some water at the end.

Leader: Good job to both our teams! We will revisit this verse later in the lesson.

2. **Sacrament Lesson**

   What you need:
   - Slides
   - Video

CG Slide: Redemptive versus non-Redemptive Sacraments

Leader: Remember last week we said there are Seven Sacraments. Four of them are redemptive—meaning they are necessary for all of us to do in order to enter the Kingdom of Heaven, and three are non-redemptive sacraments, meaning they are not required for everyone's salvation. Sacraments are a gift from God. God gave us His grace so that we could go to Heaven; we could be holy without blemish.

Today, we will discuss COMMUNION. Who can read the Key Verse for me?

CG Slide: John 6:56

Leader: Thank you—Jesus, during His time on earth talked about Communion several different times. The most well-known time is during the Last Supper when He instituted communion. But He talked about Communion previously in front of a large crowd of people who gathered to hear Him preach. He spoke today's Key Verse right after the feeding of the five thousand. Let us take a look at Jesus' words.

CG Slide: John 6:53-64 (over five slides)

Leader: Now as you can see, a lot of people were pretty offended by this and they stopped following Jesus. But Jesus did not back down. This is an essential Sacrament. Let us watch this video to see what this Sacrament means to us today and why our Church places such importance on it.

Play Video
(Key Points are:
- *Only the Holy can enter Heaven. That is why Communion is necessary and a redemptive sacrament*
- *Communion helps us become more like God*
- *Communion requires preparation*
- *Communion is the sacrament that completes all sacraments. In the Orthodox Church, we say that this is most important sacrament, because every other sacrament ends with Communion)*

3. Discussion Questions
   - Some other churches teach that Communion is only symbolic and not literally the Body and Blood of Christ. How can we be sure that Jesus was being literal?
     - Hint: Look up John 6:53-64
     - Jesus did not back down when people were offended. He did not say, "Hold up, guys! I was just speaking symbolically." He could have, but He did not.
   - Read John 13:1-8. Jesus washed the disciples' feet *before* the Last Supper—what does this teach us about preparing for Communion?
   - Why is Communion called the most important sacrament?
   - What are other names for Communion? (*Eucharist, Mystery of Mysteries, Crown of Sacraments*)

- List the benefits of partaking of Holy Communion that we discussed today.
  - *Abide in Me and I in you—to abide in Christ*
  - *To be part of the Body of Christ*
  - *For salvation*
  - *Spiritual growth*
  - *Forgiveness of sins*

4. **Olympics Practice**

   What you need:
   - Olympic practice sheet
   - Bibles

   The sheet contains verses—the teams have to look up the verses and decide if the Bible verses have to do with "taking Communion" or "preparing for Communion,"

5. **Pray and Dismiss**

Appendix IV

Teen Catered Lesson Plan of the Orthodox Creed/Ecumenical Councils[186]

Defenders of the Faith: The Holy Trinity

Bible Story/Creed Lesson: Three persons of the Holy Trinity, One God (Biblical support = various passages)
The Takeaway: We believe in the Holy Spirit, the Lord, the Life-Giver, Who proceeds from the Father, Who with the Father and the Son is worshipped and glorified.
Key Verse: "For God is not the author of confusion, but of peace." I Corinthians 14:33
Theme: Where did the Creed come from and what does it mean?

1. Opener/Ice Breaker ("Same Difference")
   - *The game today is like Scattergories. Ask for three volunteers to come up to the front of the class. Give them board markers and their own place to draw on the board.*
   - *There is a list of six objects (apple, water, ring, orange, happy, and*

---

[186] This lesson plan includes excerpts from a month long teen unit on the Origin of the Creed and the Ecumenical Councils written by the author and available at https://bridgestoorthodoxy.com/collections/crossroads (last accessed September 28, 2020).

watch). They need to draw a picture of an object that correlates with that word. (e.g. apple sauce, wedding ring, an orange crayon, a smiley face, eyes watching, etc.)
- The idea is to try to do something unique that the other two volunteers' will not put down but something that fits the category. So if they draw an apple, but someone else draws an apple, then neither person gets a point.
- If the volunteers get really stuck, audience members can raise their hands to offer ideas, but the volunteers only have one minute to complete all six drawings.
- At the end of six rounds, there are slides with pictures to show examples of various things they could have drawn—see what the volunteers came up with!
- Optional = some prize for the winning team

Leader: "Good morning all! Welcome back to our series called...

CG Slide: Defenders of the Faith

...Defenders of the Faith! If you recall, this month we are exploring a very unique time in our early church history when the Orthodox creed was formed. This occurred over the course of the Three Ecumenical Councils.

CG Slide: Three Ecumenical Councils

Ecumenical councils were universal councils where all bishops and leaders of the church would be present in order to discuss teachings of the faith to clarify and make official the church's teachings on various topics. Last week we focused on the first of these ecumenical councils: the Council of Nicaea. It was there that the first part of the Orthodox creed was formed. Today, we are moving on to the Council of Constantinople, which focused on the second part of the Creed.

CG Slide: Council of Constantinople

The heresy at the time was called the Macedonian Controversy—it focused on the Holy Trinity. This was the idea that there were three persons that make up one God. In particular, it needed clarification on the Holy Spirit. Now St. Gregory the Theologian, St. Gregory of Nyssa, and St. John Chrysostom were our Defenders of Faith. They really showed how scripture made clear that God was One and Three at the same time. And that is why our Creed looks like this:

CG Slide: Orthodox Creed

You can see that it was this council that the second part was added in and finalized: "Yes, we believe the Lord, the Life-Giver, Who proceeds from the Father, Who with the Father and the Son is worshipped and glorified, Who spoke by the prophets."

Now, how many people here are confused or have been confused about something pertaining to the Holy Trinity?

Everyone's hand should be raised. Our church fathers say that this concept is a mystery and unknowable. But what we will do today is at least get a basic understanding of what we believe and why we believe it. But first, I need you to please understand that no analogy I use today will be perfect, because that's how unknowable this mystery is.

Let's start off with a game called:

CG Slide: Same Difference

This game might help you understand very generally how something can be the same and different at the same time. I need three volunteers to come up to the board and do some drawing for me."

Pick three volunteers and explain the rules of the game. The idea is for them to draw six different pictures for the six categories, but without peeking at their neighbors' drawings. They are trying to pick a picture that is both associated with the word but also different than what the other two volunteers drew. If they get really stuck, they can ask the audience for help, but they only have one minute to draw all six drawings.

For example: if the word is "peanut," they can draw Mr. Peanut with a monocle, they can draw a peanut butter and jelly sandwich, they can draw an actual peanut, they can draw pennies because sometimes people say "working for peanuts" to mean they are working for very little, etc. the goal is to try to NOT draw the same thing as another player.

When you are ready to start the game, be sure to put a one minute timers up and also put up the list!

CG Slide: Same Difference List

Once the sixty second timer is finished you can go through the slides 7-12 to show some examples of drawings they could have done and compare to what they actually came up with. Award points as appropriate and give a round of applause to the winning volunteer.

After the game:

Leader: You all had some very creative answers! Again, no analogy is ever going to be perfect here but you can see how water can be solid ice, or liquid, or even vapor, but still be H_2O in all forms. So, intuitively, we know things can be the same but different.

CG Slide: Holy Trinity Diagram

The second Ecumenical Council and the Defenders of Faith were really focused on defending this principal about God. Yes, we believe in ONE God, but at the same time, we believe that the ONE God has THREE persons: Father, Son, and Holy Spirit.

2. Tension (Holy Trinity Council Video)

Leader: Let's take a closer look at the Holy Trinity

Play video.

After the video:

CG Slide: Holy Trinity Diagram

Leader: Okay, there was a lot of important information in this video. Let's just make sure you guys understand the basic concepts Steve talked about:
- Monotheism v. Polytheism: who can tell me what is the difference and what do we believe as Christians? (Monotheism is the belief in one God and Polytheism is the belief in many gods. As Christians, we believe in one God).
- Nature/Essence v. Person: we believe God has one united Nature or Essence but that God also has three distinct and unique persons.

- Proceeds from v. Begotten from: this just refers to how the three persons of the Holy Trinity relate to one another, but they are all God even if they are not each other—it is an incomprehensible concept so it is not a big deal if we do not completely understand everything today. It will be a life-long journey in getting to know God more and more. For today, it is enough to understand that all three persons are God united in perfect love.

Anyone else remember anything important from the video?

CG Slide: Key Verse

Keep in mind that in I Corinthians, the Bible says that God is not the author of confusion, but of peace. So if you do not understand what the words nature, essence, begotten, proceeded from mean, that is okay! If God were small enough to fit in our tiny brains, He would not be as great as He is! No analogy discussed today is going to perfectly explain it for us, no diagram is flawless—the Holy Trinity is beyond comprehension. What is really cool though, and something you are going to do in Small Groups today, is that you will be going through various Bible passages that teach us little by little about the Holy Trinity and how God makes Himself available and approachable to us through the Trinity.

In I John 4:8, we read that God is Love and we see that through the Father, Son, and Holy Spirit. When Jesus was on earth, of course it was easy to see how humans could interact with God. Then, in John 14:26-31, Jesus tells His disciples about the Holy Spirit. He called the Holy Spirit their advocate and special helper that the Father would send them after Jesus' ascension. He also tells them that they will be glad when He ascends because then they will receive the Holy Spirit. Jesus was telling us that through the Holy Spirit, we have God with us always!

You will have an opportunity to see what the Bible teaches us about the Father, the Son, and the Holy Spirit in Small Groups today. Before we break, take a look at our Defenders of the Faith for today.

CG Slide: Defenders of the Faith #3

Our early church fathers, St. Gregory the Theologian, St. Gregory of Nyssa, and St. John Chrysostom, defended the words of our Lord and what was taught about the Holy Trinity: We proclaim that the Holy Spirit is Lord, the Life-Giver, Who proceeds from the Father, Who with the Father and the Son is worshipped and glorified.

Recall what we discussed in Week 1. I do not want you to look at this series as just a history lesson; the creed is not simply a product of history. It is the work of the Holy Spirit Who is our advocate, our special helper interceding for us so that we may know a bit of the unknowable mystery of God and grow closer to Him.

3. **Discussion Questions**

- Think about our game from earlier. How can one thin be both the same and different?
    - *H_2O is a great example. H_2O refers to the composition of water, regardless if it is frozen, vapor, or in a liquid state, it will always be water. The Holy Trinity is similar—God is one in essence but takes on three distinct persons.*
- What is the difference between God as one essence but God as three distinct persons?
    - *This refers to the unity of the Holy Trinity. Father, Son, and Holy Spirit are three distinct persons but all are united perfectly in love because God is love.*
- Why do you think God took on humanity?
    - We know it was part of His plan for salvation but Jesus also talks in the verses we discussed about showing the world that Jesus loves the Father and does exactly what His Father asks of Him. He came into the world to show us God.
- In the book of Acts, we read that Jesus told the disciples to wait for the Holy Spirit.

How is the Holy Spirit different than Jesus? How the same?
- o Jesus was a physical person whereas the Holy Spirit was described as descending upon us and living inside us through the Sacraments of the church. It is another way to have the presence of God but the Holy Spirit is always with us. Jesus was not going to always be physically there.
- Do you think understating the Creed is important to your personal faith? Why or why not?
- What did you learn today about the Holy Trinity that you did not already know?

4. **Pray and Dismiss**

Appendix V

Chart Summary of the Propose Changes Discussed

Koulomzin Prong	North American Coptic Churches Today[187]	Proposed Changes
Wholeness (linking youth ministry to the practical, everyday life of the youth)	-Mainly Sunday School focused and differs from parish to parish with no universal source to pull resources from	-Diversity in programs (in and outside of Sunday) to be age appropriate and relate to social, moral, and ethical issues they face. -Materials created and continually updated by a Department of Education with a paid staff of

---

[187] Messeh, interview; Youssef, interview; Hanna, interview. These generalizations on the way many of the Coptic Orthodox parishes in North America operate are based on the author's personal knowledge as well as those confirmed in interviews with clergy. There are, however, individual parishes in North America that have implemented their own unique mechanisms into their youth ministry program(s).

		specialists in child education, development, and Orthodox Theology.
Holy Mystery "Fear of God" (helping youth experience the sacramental life of the Church and liturgical engagement through a vision developed and implemented by paid staff)	-Youth ministry is completely volunteer-run. -Programs, vision, and liturgical engagement vary from parish to parish but typically include deacon classes, choir, and Coptic hymn lessons.	-Invest in at least one paid staff member who will develop and implement a cohesive vision for youth ministry and will create programs in and out of Sunday to better experience the mystery of God. -The paid leader should be empowered to select and equip volunteers with the blessing of the priest.
Reality of God (helping youth experience the living	-Volunteers (servants) take their role seriously and many parishes	-Allow volunteers to shadow the program before committing and the commitment should be finite (e.g., one year).

God through the volunteers)	have a pre-servants program that must be completed before they can serve. -Actual programs vary by parish or diocese, but many Coptic Churches do spiritual retreats in addition to Sunday school. -While some diocese have a Sunday school topic-guide to follow, volunteers are	-Volunteer selection should be focused on finding spiritual role models. -Equip the volunteers with detailed lesson plans and content of the programs so that the quality stays cohesive and consistent.

	required to write their own lesson plans.	
Body of Christ (helping youth discover their unique place in the Body of Christ through meaningful programs)	-Largely Sunday school focused, but some parishes have other programs such as sports leagues, youth groups, or summer competitions.	-Create meaningful and comprehensive programs both in and out outside of Sunday to help kids find out their unique passions and talents. -More non-Sunday programs such as community service, sports, mentorship, and fun fellowship time should be introduced.
Religious Education (fostering spiritual growth of youth by partnering the Church with parents)	-Largely Sunday school focused, with little to no family participation. -Parents have their	-Create communication mechanisms and a partnership with parents and youth ministry so that they know what their kids are learning and are equipped to carry the lesson home.

	own adult sermons but typically are not involved in anything Sunday school related.	-Create family programs/resources to assist parents with their child's spiritual education at home.

Bibliography

"252 Kids Curriculum." Orange. http://www.252kidscurriculum.com (accessed September 18, 2018).

"A Vision on Youth Ministry." Orthodox Church in America. https://www.oca.org/the-hub/about-youth-ministry/a-vision-on-youth-ministry (accessed September 11, 2018).

Allen, Joseph J. *The Ministry of the Church: Image of Pastoral Care.* Yonkers: SVS Press, 1986.

Anderson, Michael. "Is Your Area Meeting the Needs of Your Youth?" *Orthodox Church in America.* https://oca.org/the-hub/about-youth-ministry/is-your-area-meeting-the-needs-of-your-youth (accessed September 11, 2018).

Anderson, Michael. "Our Youth Need You." *Orthodox Church in America.* https://oca.org/the-hub/study-guides/our-youth-need-you1 (accessed September 10, 2018).

Antiochian Orthodox Christian Archdiocese of North America. "The Department of Christian Education." http://ww1.antiochian.org/christianeducation (accessed September 10, 2018).

Bishop Moussa. "How to Speak to Youth?" Cairo: Bishopric of Youth, 2002.

Bishop Moussa. "Youth Concerns: Questions and Answers." Cairo: Bishopric of Youth, 2007.

Bishop Serapion. "Ninth Grade." *Sunday School Program of the Coptic Orthodox Church, Diocese of Los Angeles, Southern California, and Hawaii.* August 27, 1999.

Bishop Suriel. *Habib Girgis: Coptic Educator and a Light in the Darkness.* Yonkers: SVS Press, 2017.

Bishop Youssef. *Adapting to a New Place Called Home.* Sandia: St. Mary and St. Moses Abbey Press, 2016.

Bishoy, Shenouda. *Topics for Christian Youth.* Chicago: St. Mark & St. Bishoy Coptic Orthodox Church, 1987.

Boojamra, John L. *Foundations for Christian Education.* Yonkers: SVS Press, 1989.

Breck, John. *The Sacred Gift of Life.* Yonkers: SVS Press, 2000.

Bridges to Orthodoxy. http://www.bridgestoorthodoxy.com (last accessed September 28, 2020).

Coptic Orthodox Church of Archangel Raphael and St. John the Beloved of Chapel Hill, North Carolina. "Sunday School Curriculum." http://www.chapelhillcoptic.net/dnn/en-us/churchservices/curriculum.aspx (accessed March 12, 2018).

Coptic Orthodox Diocese of Los Angeles, Southern California, and Hawaii. "About Us/Mahragan al-Keraza." http://www.ysc-keraza.org/about-us/mahragan-al-keraza/ (accessed September 10, 2018).

Coptic Orthodox Diocese of the Southern United States. "Sunday School Curriculum." https://www.suscopts.org/ssc (accessed March 12, 2018).

Erikson, Erik H. *Identity Youth and Crisis*. New York: W.W. Norton& Company, 1994.

Fields, Doug. *Purpose Driven Youth Ministry: Nine Essential Foundations for Healthy Growth*. Grand Rapids: Zondervan Academic, 1998.

Gaskins, Pearl. *I Believe In…* Chicago: Cricket Books, 2004.

Greek Orthodox Archdiocese of America. "Department of Religious Education." https://www.goarch.org/departments/religioused (accessed September 10, 2018).

Harakas, Stanley S. *Contemporary Moral Issues Facing the Orthodox Christian*. Minneapolis: Light & Life Publishing, 1982.

Harakas, Stanley S. *Living the Faith: The Praxis of Eastern Orthodox Ethics*. Minneapolis: Light & Life Publishing, 1982.

Havrilak, Gregory. "Youth Ministry: A Foundation." *Orthodox Church in America*. https://oca.org/the-hub/leader-info-about-youth-ministry/youth-ministry-a-foundation1 (accessed September 10, 2018).

Hybels, Bill. *The Volunteer Revolution: Unleashing the Power of Everybody*. Grand Rapids: Zondervan Academic, 2004.

Joseph, Thomas. "Youth Formation." Symposium, https://teensoyo.org/youth-formation/ (accessed August 17, 2018).

Koulomzin, Sophie. "Children and Christian Education." *Orthodox Church in America*. https://oca.org/the-hub/leader-info-youth-ministry/children-and-christian-education1 (accessed September 10, 2018).

Koulmozin, Sophie. *Our Church and Our Children*. Yonkers: SVS Press, 2004.

Magdalen, Sister. *Children in the Church Today: An Orthodox Perspective*. Yonkers: SVS Press, 1991.

Morgan, Tony and Tim Stevens. *Simply Strategic Volunteers: Empowering People for Ministry*. Loveland: Group Publishing, 2005.

Purpura, Joseph F. *Moral and Ethical Issues: Confronting Orthodox Christian Teens Across North America*. 1st Books Library, 2002.

Purpura, Joseph F. "Youth Formation." Symposium. https://teensoyo.org/youth-formation/ (accessed August 17, 2018).

Shams el-Din, Mai. "Copts and Egypt's National Game: We'll Call You Back Later." *Navigate*. https://www.madamasr.com/en/2017/07/20/feature/society/copts-and-egypts-national-game-well-call-you-back-later/ (accessed December 11, 2017).

"The Church." Orthodox Church in America. https://oca.org/orthodoxy/the-orthodox-faith/spirituality/orthodox-spirituality/the-church (accessed September 11. 2018).

St. Mary and St. Athanasius Coptic Orthodox Church. "The PEP Talks." http://www.thePEPTALKS.org (accessed September 11, 2018).

St. Timothy and St. Athanasius Coptic Orthodox Church. "Parent Resource Page." http://stsa.church/parents (accessed August 17, 2018).

Sorial, Michael. *Incarnational Exodus*. St. Cyril of Alexandria Orthodox Society Press, 2014.

Strommen, Merton P. *Five Cries of Youth*. San Francisco: Harper & Row, 1979.

Think Orange. "XP3 Students." http://thinkorange.com/xp3s/ (accessed September 18, 2018).

Youth Bishopric. "Mission Statement." http://youthbishopric.com/ (accessed August 14, 2018).

About the Author

Shereen M. Marcus is a wife, mother of two boys, and works full time as a Veterans Law Judge (VLJ) for the Board of Veterans' Appeals. She earned her JD from George Washington University. Her legal career spans nearly two decades, to include government contracts, commercial litigation, veterans law, appellate litigation, and, now, as a Veterans Law Judge. Concurrently, she has been an advocate for reforming youth ministry in Orthodox churches in North America for many years. Starting off with a few ideas, some writing ability, and a knack for kid silliness, Shereen did independent research into various youth ministry efforts and methodologies while writing youth Christian education materials for her local parish. She furthered her work by competing a Master's degree in Orthodox Theology from the Antiochian House of Studies in conjunction with the University of Balamand in Lebanon. From there, she took her materials to a bigger platform by launching *Bridges to Orthodoxy* in January 2020. She continues to write Christian education materials and lecture on youth ministry efforts and methodologies. You can find her work on Christian education at www.bridgestoorthodoxy.com.

www.ingramcontent.com/pod-product-compliance
Lightning Source LLC
Chambersburg PA
CBHW030525080526
44586CB00011B/331